I was a teenage worrier

www.kidsatrandomhouse.co.uk

I was a teenage worrier

Written and Illustrated by
Ros Asquith as Letty Chubb

CORGI BOOKS

I WAS A TEENAGE WORRIER
A CORGI BOOK 0552555568

First published in Great Britain
by Piccadilly Press Ltd 1992
Corgi edition first published 1994

Corgi edition revised and reissued 2005

Papers used by Random House Children's Books are natural,
recyclable products made from wood grown in sustainable forests.
The manufacturing processes conform to the environmental
regulations of the country of origin.

Set in 12pt Sabon by
Falcon Oast Graphic Art

Corgi Books are published by
Random House Children's Books,
61–63 Uxbridge Road, London W5 5SA,
a division of The Random House Group Ltd,
in Australia by Random House Australia (Pty) Ltd,
20 Alfred Street, Milsons Point, Sydney, NSW 2061, Australia,
in New Zealand by Random House New Zealand Ltd,
18 Poland Road, Glenfield, Auckland 10, New Zealand,
and in South Africa by Random House (Pty) Ltd,
Endulini, 5A Jubilee Road, Parktown 2193, South Africa

THE RANDOM HOUSE GROUP Limited Reg. No. 954009
www.kidsatrandomhouse.co.uk

A CIP catalogue record for this book is available from the British Library.

Printed and bound in Great Britain by
Cox & Wyman Ltd, Reading, Berkshire.

For teenage worriers everywhere.
And with special thanks to John.

CONTENTS

phew

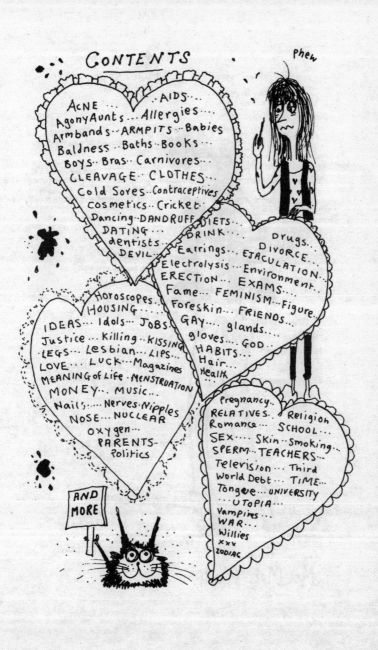

AND MORE

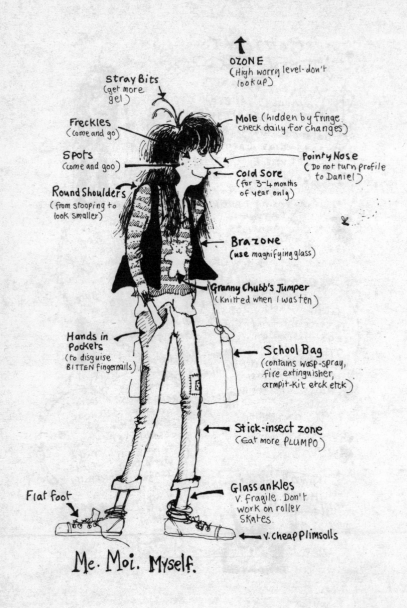

OZONE
(High worry level- don't look up)

Stray Bits
(get more gel)

Freckles
(come and go)

Mole (hidden by fringe, check daily for changes)

Spots
(come and goo)

Pointy Nose
(Do not turn profile to Daniel)

Cold Sore
(for 3-4 months of year only)

Round Shoulders
(from stooping to look smaller)

Brazone
(use magnifying glass)

Granny Chubb's Jumper
(Knitted when I was ten)

Hands in Pockets
(to disguise BITTEN fingernails)

School Bag
(contains wasp-spray, fire extinguisher, armpit-kit etck etck)

Stick-insect zone
(Eat more PLUMPO)

Glass ankles
v. fragile. Don't work on roller skates.

Flat foot

v. cheap Plimsolls

Me. Moi. Myself.

Pokey House
Small St
London
England
Little Britain
Europe (ho ho)
The World
The Solar System
The Galaxy
The Universe
Infinity

Dear Reader,

*Do you know how it feels to be Really
WORRIED? When your palms feel like frogspawn,
your armpits like hot margarine, your head as if a
Heavy Metal Band is rehearsing inside it? Well, this
is a book about HOW NOT TO WORRY (ho ho,
pull the other one, what do I know, etck) so if any
of the above rings a bell with you then I hope this
slim volume will be the BUSINESS.*

*Not that I haven't been really Worried about
writing it. The more you write a book on this
subject, the more you realize how much there is to
WORRY ABOUT and what started as some GCSE
coursework (groan) on the v. fascinating subject of
SUPERSTITIONS has grown into this Money-
spinning Pot-Boiler (er, I mean v. Important self-help
book for the citizens of the Future).*

*Anyway, if I can conquer my Worries (being the
biggest Worrier on Planet Earth) then you can too.*

I have been a Teenager for over two years so I

should know. I wish someone had told me about all this stuff when I was 10. Then I would be able to traverse a perfectly normal pavement without worrying about treading on the cracks (boo hoo, whinge, GROW UP, etck).

Anyway, I am doing this Great Work as an ALPHABET and I will try to deal with the MAIN WORRIES AFFECTING US TEENAGERS TODAY. Like SPOTS, WILLY SIZE (yes boys, if yours is bigger than fourteen inches you don't have to worry. Just my little joke), How-to-look-as-if-you-don't-care-when-your-best-friend-gets-off-with-the-only-one-you'll-ever-lurve (sob, violins, Kleenex, etck), CAREERS (and how long the queue is to put your name down for one), and the MEANING OF LIFE – right on top of the pile for causing anguished palpitations, unfinished home-work, poetry-writing and playing with your gentiles (N.B. Check spelling before handing book in). Don't think that if you turn to WILLIES or the MEANING OF LIFE you don't have to read the rest though, as Willies pop up everywhere and you can't find them all by browsing in a bookshop, so don't be such a cheapskate.

I will leave out the really NIGGLY worries like BISCUITS (my aunt used to worry that if she took the fancy ones off a plate then the plain ones would feel lonely) and LINO (my little brother Benjy is v. scared of our kitchen floor), as I feel these are MINORITY Worries. Also v.v. big Worries, like whether the sun will turn into a

2

White Dwarf next week and what would happen
to my Teacher (who is a bit of a white dwarf herself)
if it did.

But I am Worried that I might have left out a
really Important Worry (big OR little) that is really
really Worrying YOU. If so, dear Reader, please
write to me and I will try to persuade my publisher
(blush) to put it in the next edition of this book
(visions of flame, gory, etck).

Meanwhile please buy this book so I can get
v. rich. I mean so you can stop WORRYING and
start LIVING.

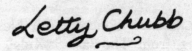

THINGS YOU MIGHT LIKE TO KNOW ABOUT ME BEFORE YOU SPEND YOUR BOOK TOKEN:

NAME: Scarlett Jane Chubb
AGE: 15 years 2 months

HEIGHT: 5' 8½" and still growing (sob sob).
WEIGHT: 7 stone (in all my clothes with Doc Martens ironclad boots on).
HAIR: Dark mouse. Long, straight, looks like bowl of wholewheat spaghetti tipped on head.

NICKNAMES: Concorde (my Nose . . .), Chubby, Plug (from 'The Bash St Kids', OF COURSE).
My FRENDZ call me Letty.

My family all have red hair except me. Many people say the Red-Haired are Mad and since I'm the only Mouse and they called me Scarlett – this proves it.

To be called Scarlett is a Cross I Bear for my whole life. My Posh Gran was obsessed with a film called *Gone With the Wind*, which is not an ad for bicarbonate of soda but a V. famous Classic about a crafty cow called Scarlett O'Hara who knew how to wind men around her little finger, including her butler.

My Big Brother ended up with Ashley (eek) and we CAMPAIGNED to stop my mother calling my little brother Rhett (cringe).

I am going to be a world famous Film Director. I am V. Thin and eat PLUMPO but it doesn't work. I get no sympathy because all my friends are on diets.

My interests are Films, Art, Poetry, Photog. And Horses. And, more recently, Boys. Or rather, Boy. There is only one for me and if I can't have him I may become a nun instead of a Film Director.

On the whole I prefer horses to boys. They have nicer eyes and are more intelligent. I made the mistake of telling one of my horrible friends this and they said it's because horses have got bigger willies, which just shows you what kind of people I have to hang about with to avoid being A Woman Alone.

I stoop and wear flat shoes always. My spindly form means I will never be heart high to a man and look up at him adoringly, but this is the 21st century so WHO CARES? (I do.)

A quick word about the other inhabitants of my life and work:

BROTHER 1

NAME: Ashley Michael Chubb
AGE: 18
Tall, thin, dark auburn hair extravagantly handsome, absurdly clever (yeech), Scholarship to Oxford (Brains-and-Beauty, lash, moan). Plans to

be a doctor and help poor people, if there are any left alive by the time he qualifies. Ha! Too good to be true, etck etck, grrrrr. There is a constant stream of girls outside our house Baying at the Moon on his account. Grandad Gosling paid for his education, but Hard Times came before the money filtered down to me. What I say is, if a State Education is good enough for 97% of the Nation's Offspring, it's good enough for me.

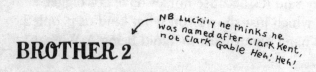

NB Luckily he thinks he was named after Clark Kent, not Clark Gable. Heh! Heh!

BROTHER 2

NAME: Benjamin Clark Chubb (Benjy)
AGE: 5
Looks like a laughing apple with freckles, and of course the apple of everyone's eye (ahh BLESS!). I PRETEND I don't like him, because it's UnKool to be soppy about a little brother. Cootchy-coo. Benjy was what is called a 'mistake'. My father ran off with a trapeze artist when I was 10, came back three weeks later to make it up to my mum and lo! Along came Benjy. My Mother likes to remind him of this two or three times a week (not Benjy, my Dad). She has never mentioned it to Benjy because she worries that Benjy would prefer a trapeze artist for a mum to someone who groans about climbing the stairs to the loo.

Benjy has unleashed the CHILD in me which is
v. important according to Dr Fred Freud,
psychotherapist to the stars.

MOTHER

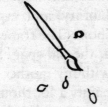

NAME: Alice Constance Gosling
AGE: Forty-something
BACKGROUND: Stinking Rich and Posh with it. Posh
stinking-rich people are different e.g. they do mad
things and end up in *Harpers and Queen* magazine
while everyone else does mad things and ends up in
the nick. (They are let out later to Roam Free and
bite the heads off Infants. This is called Scaring the
Community.) Being rich means you can be v. cross
and rude because you don't have to lick anybody's
you-know-what, so V. Rich people avoid contact
with humans and spend most of their time with
animals instead. If any socializing with people who
Aren't Like Them (tradesmen, children, etck) has to
be done they pay slaves to do it.

Ergo (this is Latin and proves my Mastermind-
type general knowledge), my mother was brought
up by a Nanny and hardly SAW her parents.
Judging by her Mother, maybe she was lucky. She
had her own pony and about eight thousand dogs
(envy, envy). She never learnt to cook or anything
and misses one of those uncomplaining machines

that suck up dust, called a Cleaner, so she's always nagging us about tidiness. She's v. tidy herself, because if anything is out of place it's one more *exhausting* thing to have to do to find it.

But now she has to have a JOB (in the Kiddies' Library) and, ergo, she hardly ever remembers to shop. (The trapeze artist was apparently very good at the old spag. bog, which is an even sorer point with my mother than the spangly leotard.) She paints a lot though (having sacrificed her artistic career on the altar of childbearing Etck Etck, whinge, boo hoo) and would rather do that than lurch about in the kitchen burning herself and drowning sprouts. Of course I support her in this. A woman's place is in the World, I say. But I need to eat since I am built like a sockful of clothespegs, so there is a conflict. Aaargh, squirm, wring, etck.

FATHER

NAME: Leonard Anthony Chubb
AGE: Fifty-something
BACKGROUND: Church mouse. Mum a cleaner, Dad a builder.

My father is a Writer with a capital W and thus spends a lot of his time doing Research i.e. filling the house with millions of newspapers and maga-zines constituting a V. Worrying Fire Hazard. He swept my Mother off her feet (swoon swoon) when he had just written his first novel *MOVING ON* about a poor country boy made good in London but at Odds with Society and Rejected by his Peers. Etck whinge. V. sad.

He won literary prizes, was the toast of London and has been living off the toast ever since, now v. stale. It has been 22 years. He does a lot of articles (mainly on Do-It-Yourself) for magazines and papers, though. He is V. Left Wing. His only Worry is his next novel. When it's finished, he says, we'll all live in a mansion with a swimming pool and be champagne socialists inviting poor people round for creative writing classes.

PETS

HORACE: Benjy's gerbil. Needs a big lavvy roll supply. Granny Chubb obliges. Goes round on a wheel all day.

ROVER: My cat. I have had her since before I knew I was allergic. She is old and not well, but can still open the fridge, so My Father barricades it with bricks so none of us can open the fridge except him, which is OK because there's never anything in it except cans of Old Bastard Premium Ale or whatever it is. Ha! Rover sleeps on my bed, which is one of the reasons I sneeze all the time.

My Darling Father
("at work"
ho ho)

My Darling Mother
(deciding whether
Toulouse Lautrec
understood Women)

Horace
(going
round)

Accident
waiting
to Happen

Ye Chubbe Householde.

FRENDZ

BEST FRIEND: Hazel Williams
Nearly 16 and V. Gorgeous. Makes Beyoncé look
like Jonathan Woss. Boys have noticed this, groan
whinge. We have been best friends since we were at
Primary School when all we did was play with
model horses, but I think we may be growing apart
(sob sob) because her parents moved her from
Sluggs Comprehensive to St Mary's Academy
which costs an arm and a leg but which they think
removes her from the clutches of Boys, those Evil
Sex Machines From Hell.

OTHER BEST FRIEND: Aggy Parsons
15 and fat. She is in my class at Sluggs. Also short-
sighted and hates her glasses, so her only ambition
is to save enough money to buy a contact lens to

add to the one she found on the floor of the public loo outside the Job Centre.

Her father is Black and her mother (of Whom we Do Not Speak) was White and ran off with the postman. I often try to talk to her about the oppression of Being Black in a Racist Society, but she is more interested in Physics. Always dieting, but very clever INDEED and wants to be a scientist. Comes to photography class with me on Thursdays, blames glasses for never having kissed a boy and is v.v. worried about this. Gets occasional letters from her Mum (probably free delivery).

BOYFRIENDS

Daniel Hope
Daniel is 17. He is tall and dead gorgeous, a cross between Brad Pitt, David Beckham and Justin Timberlake but with hair the colour of wet sand at sunset and eyes the colour of Smarties (no, not the red ones, the blue ones, swoon). I lost my heart to him three months, two weeks and four days ago. He is at school with Hazel's brother. It is a mega mega dead swish boarding school, but he is Not Like That. He understands the struggles of ordinary working people like myself. He read *Moving On* when he was 13 and thinks my Dad is great. I have never met any-one else under 40 who's read it. I may as well admit

that nothing of a carnal nature has passed between Daniel and me, but I have not been so interested in horses since our Historic Meeting. He asked Hazel if I would be at her 16th Birthday Party and I feel that something is bound to happen between us soon.

Brian Bolt

Brian, known as Brain, is gangly with legs like fuse wire and rather a spotty complexion which is clearing up, I hope. I am fond of him in a way but The Spark Is Not There and I fear he is fonder of me. Last Feb I got a Valentine card that was so big the postman had to leave it with a neighbour. And it was signed A. Nony Mouse in Brian's perfect copperplate hand. (CRINGE.) I am trying hard to get him together with Aggy. My soul is Otherwise Engaged.

GRANDPARENTS

Granny Gosling

My mother's mother. Talks like the Queen's speech at Christmas. I used to call her Chandelier Tonsils but since she had a throat operation for Something Nasty I have considered that Bad Taste. She communicates on the subject of Falling Standards by thrice weekly illegible letters to my mother. But she only ever sends v. small presents. She is in something called 'reduced circumstances'.

Granny Chubb
My father's mother. Was a cleaner for 52 years.
Old habits die hard so your plate can disappear
between mouthfuls if you don't hang on to it with
your other hand. Cleans her own windows every
day so her neighbours think she's spying on them.
Otherwise sane and V. Nice. Does not consider my
mother a Good Housewife (tsk Etck).

Grandfathers
Sadly no longer with us.

NB

Before I start, I ought to point out two little
eccentricities I have: first, I do not at time of writing
have a MOBILE. I think I may be the last teenager
in UK or even werld who does not (perlease write to
me if you are in the same boat) but I must be honest
and admit I have had two. My first was nicked by
some rude boys and the second I left on the bus.

My adored parents have put their feet down on
this one but I have now nearly saved enough for a
pay-as-you-go, as life is a mere incomplete shadow
of glume without a mobile . . . (although it does
stop me texting Daniel every five mins).

Second, I cannot bring myself to write or say
one particular word. It is a word about dying and

it rhymes with 'breath'. I always use 'banana' instead. Since I can't conquer this, you might as well know about it. Otherwise you will not know what I'm talking about. I'll avoid it as much as poss.

Rover has no conception of Impending Doom

CHAPTER ONE (A)

*August. TWO weeks to go Till Hazel's Party . . .
(Yippeeeee tremble). Two weeks and two days to
go till school (groan grr).*

*I am spending a bit longer than usual on my
appearance and then walking the long way round
to the shops in case I might bump into Daniel,
but no luck so far (sob). Aggy and I have entered
our photos for a newspaper competition – first
prize a digital camera and a day with Arty
Photographer, Hendon Snap. Yahooo! Fingers
crossed. But I am worried that Aggy's tender
spirit will be crushed if I win. I fear she has NO
CHANCE since she has sent in a wacky photo-
montage of her own head superimposed on a
diagram of the collision paths of neutrinos or
something. I don't see how she can compete with
my moving Human Destiny pictures of Granny
Chubb asleep with a bottle of Guinness and her
false teeth out.*

*I have been searching for a padded bra. I know
it's silly, but I am getting nervy about Hazel's party
(twitch, tremble). Also Worried about Granny
Chubb (flu) and Rover (cat flu). Gave Granny
Chubb tin of KITTY BLISS in error but she said
it's better than what she normally eats. Wish I*

could have got a snap of her eating it to add to Human Destiny portfolio. Ashley has gone to Oxford and my mother is moping because the ceiling's fallen down in the kitchen. My father hasn't replaced it as it's given him an idea for an article on mould (or was it mouldings?) and he's doing on-site research. She thought he could have chosen another room but they are all stuffed with newspapers.

Now I start my A–Z of Worry, roll on drums, tremble, twitch, Etck.

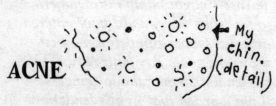

ACNE

One of Yoof's BIGGEST Worries and rightly Number One Worry in this Alphabet. It is the worst form of those excrescences otherwise known as Spots, Pimples, Plukes, Zits, Etck Etck. The only real remedy is getting older, which you can't help doing (you hope).

My Father had Real Acne and though his face today is a Tube Map of broken veins, razor cuts, wrinkles, crow's feet, stubble and bits of white emulsion, there is not a ZIT to be seen. So THERE. Chinese herbs are the latest cure but must be used with care, so badger your Doctor. Doctor Your Badger also, to convince yourself you are a Worthwhile Person (ha!).

BOYZ get spots worse

I'll cover spots here, because you have to cover spots before they cover you. I get them a lot. They always come just before a party, or a date. (See also COLD SORES.) The ones on the tip of your nose are the worst. If they appear on a small nose they look in the mirror as if a Scud missile has shot up your nostril and blown a hole in your hooter from the inside. If they appear on a large nose then hooter and pluke merge to form a Gigantic Red Alien that looks as if it has landed on your face and is about to Eat Your Head. Either way, they look worse to the Victim, because other people are too worried about what they look like to worry much about you.

TIP: NEVER cover a spot, pimple, pluke or zit with a plaster. A boy once asked me out when he had a boil the size of Vesuvius on his nose, with a little

19

shine ooze
throb
suppurate
glow
fester
pulsate

The Beezer Pluke:
How it appears to you

The Beezer Pluke:
How it appears to others

round plaster bobbing up and down on the end of
it so it looked as if it was wearing a sunhat, and
too late at that. Still, I suppose if I had liked him
I would have said Yes.

NB. My Father's Dictionary of Quotations only
reveals ONE about Spots. 'Out, out, damned Spot'
by Shakespeare. This proves that Prince Charles
was right to say The Bard is Relevant to us
Teenagers Today.

AGONY AUNTS

Money for old rope dept.
Sample Letter:

Dear Cindy,
I am in love with my History teacher. He is
forty-five, married with four children and his eyes

are Spring Skies with Gathering Storms around the edges. He knows everything there is to know about the History Of The World and he has asked me over to his house on Friday to discuss The Enlightenment. His wife, who doesn't understand him, is away with the kids. He says I make him feel A Teenager Again, and he is just waiting till the two-year-old has grown up and then he will get a Divorce. Meantime, can you advise me on contraception?
Yours sincerely,
Patsy (14½)

Dear Patsy,
    Forget this selfish monster immediately. Also, you are under age for sex. Find a boy your own age for sex, I mean, to be friends with. Or how about some new interests? Or a pet? I enclose my booklets on New Interests and Pets.

I feel more sympathetic to some scribes . . .

. . . than others

Etck Etck. You can write these answers yourself. I have only written about two dozen letters to Agony Aunts, which, considering how Worried I am about everything, is not many. The trouble is, Agony Aunts are not Truly Sensitive about your SOUL. If you think how Patsy's really feeling, taking a goldfish ice-skating won't Mend The Heartache will it?

Though I am trying hard to wean myself off them, I do still work out letters to Problem Pages in the small hours of the morning. I haven't actually sent one off now for two and a half months, though, ever since I had that very BIG Worry about BRAS, but I'll tell you more about that later.

AIDS

It's amazing how few people seem to be really
Worried about AIDS. AIDS kills you, it's spreading,
and you get it from Sex, so although I know I am a
Worrier, it strikes me as weird that a lot of girls as
well as boys are going on as if AIDS didn't exist.
Especially since if you use condoms for their True
Purpose rather than making water bombs like
Benjy, you cut the risk of catching AIDS a lot. This
is called SAFER SEX. Other forms of Safer Sex
include Kissing, Fondling and generally Fiddling
About without Doing It (phew, steam), going to
bed with someone to discuss Structuralism, or
reading a book by Jackie Collins. What I have
found out is you can't possibly catch the HIV virus,
which causes AIDS, from sharing a meal off a loo
seat (sorry, there should have been a comma in
there), shaking hands, hugging and all that. The
virus is v.v. fragile outside the human body.

My parents Worried about something called VD,
which meant you had to wear a bag over your
head with a false moustache painted on it when
going to the hospital. I think My Mother is sorry
that Teenage Lurve is blighted by the spread of
AIDS, but is horrified that nobody I know is as
worried about AIDS as she and the Govt think we
ought to be.

Worrying about AIDS can make you really
worried about SEX and sometimes I think I might

23

just be a Nun, or even stay a virgin till they find a cure. Virgins are becoming fashionable again, although I wouldn't like to marry one myself. I might as well admit I haven't DONE IT this early on so you know who you're dealing with. Hazel is another matter though, which I'll tell you about in the SEX section (but don't cheat and turn to it without reading the rest or you'll go blind).

Everyone *should* Worry about AIDS anyway, but the best thing to do is get a good book about STDs (Sexually Transmitted Diseases) from the Library and you can have a really good Worry and learn how to take care of yourself at the same time. The main thing is, though people don't always realize it, boys don't only get it from other boys (Gay Plague Shock Horror Panic Perverts Etck Etck) but they can get it from girls and girls can get it from boys so that has most forms of Doing It covered except Girls with Girls, which is pretty low in the AIDS stakes. Only a V. Small minority of the population, however, think the latter is the answer to stopping AIDS. I think it would be more fun to be a Lesbian than a Nun though I'm sure many Happy Nuns will disagree.

I got out a book that said 'Most experts believe that it is safe to kiss' (???!!!!) but since AIDS is only passed in blood products, you'd have to have sores or cuts in or around your mouth for it to be a Risk. You'd need literally BUCKETS of saliva to pass it on, so unless you're a V. Messy Kisser, you don't have to spit in a glass and hold it up to the light before you kiss somebody.

A friend of my Big Brother Ashley died of AIDS last Christmas. He was V. Brave about it, but he said he only forget to use condoms once and that was enough. I didn't like to admit I had never had to ask anyone to use one yet. This boy said the thing that drove him crazy was when the papers go on about INNOCENT victims. As if it's anyone's FAULT they got AIDS. I miss him, and I feel V. Sorry for his boyfriend and parents. But I think he has helped me worry about this in a more SENSIBLE way, which is more than I can say about most of the things in this book.

But I also found out that although drugs can help hugely with HIV, there is no cure for AIDS. (I really hope they find one by the time I'm Doing It.) And that if you're unlucky enough to have a drug habit, don't share needles with *anybody* or you've Had It.

I do sometimes Worry about Daniel as the man most likely to Awaken Me As A Woman (yeech, per-*yuke*). I wonder if he's had the test? Could I bring myself to ask him? I suppose I should wait until he's asked me out properly, before I bring it up.

NB. Always use water-based lubricants or spermi-cides as oily ones – even hand creams – can destroy condoms (arg).

ALLERGIES

I sneeze about 54,000 times every morning between April and September. This is hay fever, caused by pollen in the air, and it is a Big Pain, especially when you are moving Rapturously towards your One True Lurve and then blow him into next week with a salvo of snot, bits of cheese sandwich, fillings, Etck.

One of My Father's favourite jokes is to say 'Does your nose run and your feet smell? Then you're built upside down.' Ha! Just as well he is not staking his Comeback on being a Comic Novelist.

NB:
Avoid sudden movements when
a bee or wasp approaches

There's a lot of stuff you can take for hay fever and most of it sends you to sleep which is a v. good excuse for avoiding washing up, failing exams, etck etck.

But if you're an allergic sort of person there's plenty of other stuff to Worry about. I've had tests for LIFE THREATENING allergies to bees, wasps, house mites, pollen, dogs, cats, horses (only V. Mild, luckily) and about ten other things I've forgotten.

NB. Shakespeare again: 'Where the Bee sucks there suck I.' Think again, Prince of Wales.

ARMBANDS

If you are 10, and can swim, you don't need them. If you have a small sibling who can't, you may be interested to know that a recent survey said a lot of armbands LET THE AIR OUT. Some small siblings are so fat you can't get the armbands on in the first place. I have tried putting them on Benjy when deflated (the armbands that is, Benjy is never deflated) and blowing them up afterwards but Benjy went a bit blue so I stopped.

TIP: Feel free to analyse the above and use in accordance with your relationship with your sibling.

ARMPITS

There are two main armpit Worries: SMELL and HAIR.

It is v. unfair that boys and men never seem to worry about shaving their armpits unless they are dressing up as women. Now you may not have any hair under your arms, but one day you will. If you are a girl, you may grow up to fear The Invasion Of The Killer Armwigs.

I should like to say that this is completely unnecessary. It is absolutely natural for women to have hair there and I wholly agree with G. Greer in asking why should we Grovel to Stereotypical images of Female Beauty Etck? But when every SINGLE picture of a woman in a bathing suit or a sleeveless dress shows hairless armpits, you'd have to be a very strong character INDEED not to have a Little Worry.

I have tried various techniques to overcome this Worry, including Long Sleeves (Hot, esp. in Greenhouse Effect), Keeping Arms To Sides (Difficult re Sports, Sex and Surrendering to Urban Guerrillas), Waxing (Painful), Depilatory Creams (V. Pongy and don't get the Thick Bits In The Middle) and Shaving (causes Scrubbing Brush Effect).

So, since I haven't been able to work out a 100% fail-safe solution to this, I am going to launch CHAP (The Campaign for Hairy Arm Pits),

Invasion of the KiLLER Armwigs!

which will re-educate The Public that their Armpits
Can Be Charmpits. I will fake Elizabethan Love
Poems devoted to these intoxicating Caverns of
Paradise, start a CHAP-RAP band who play with
their instruments held over their heads.
Hairdressers will offer Mohican armpits, Braided
armpits, Rainbow armpits. (It also means less Hair
Waste to create another Ecological Timebomb.
Where do all the hair-clippings GO?)

TIP: As for SMELL. I find three thick lots of foaming soap plus deodorant six times daily does the trick (roll-on of course to protect ozone layer etck).

CHAPTER TWO (B)

(ONE week to go till Hazel's Party (twitch, tremble).)
We are eating plaster dust with every meal.
I am getting a COLD SORE on my top lip, which
I am pouring buckets of surgical spirit on (argh).
My mother found it and thought it was a designer
drug. How could My Only Mother In The World
THINK such a thing?!

I am feeling V. Sympatico with My Father just
now as I am understanding how lonely is the life of
a writer. I have not found a decent bra (see below)
and I feel a poem on the subject coming on.

Benjy has got chicken pox. My mother says I
have had it but I am wearing a scarf round my
mouth just in case. If I got the pox before the party
I would DIE. Went riding (payment for ten hours
mucking out) but the horse reminded me of Daniel.
Sang 'Four Legged Friend' to it and it threw me
into a hedge. Hope this isn't an OMEN. On with
the BEEEEEEZZZ.

BABIES

It amazes me in this day and age how many girls
seem to be obsessed with having babies. Lisa in

Your dream incy-wincy Baba

. . . the Real Thing

Year 10 had one so she could get a council flat. She ended up in a horrible Bed and Breakfast though, and said she found out that the reason they're called that is because the last person leaves their breakfast in the bed, usually after they've eaten it (yeech, per-yuke Etck Etck).

Still, you have to get used to this sort of environment anyway, because babies leave a lot of this kind of stuff around the place themselves. Personally, babies are too pukey and smelly and squashy and noisy for me. However, I make an exception about Benjy (aaah BLESS!), who has always been cuddly, curly, cute Etck Etck. A major Worry of mine is how not to have them before 26, and I think the best way of ENSURING that is not to have any sex. If I can't hold out till then I will use a cap, a coil and the pill all at once. If The Boy of My Dreams uses condoms too it should be OK.

It is also worth bearing in mind that hardly any boys want babies. 'Single parent' is a fashionable phrase just now. I have noticed that it almost always means single mother.

BALDNESS

Boys Worry a lot about this. It is so Worrying for them that they have decided that if they go bald it means they are more VIRILE, to compensate. Boys as young as 12 inspect their hairlines and look gloomily at the way their fathers have combed two or three lonely hairs from behind their right ears over to their left eyebrows and stuck them down with gel mixed with wallpaper paste.

> **TIP:** Do not waste your Saturday-job money
> on hair restorers. And remember that it is now
> cool to be a baldy.

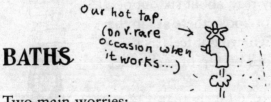

Our hot tap.
(on v. rare
occasion when
it works...)

BATHS

Two main worries:
1) Can you get as many as you need?
2) Would you want your friends to see your Bathroom?

My father keeps turning the heating off to economize and says he went to the public bath once a week if he was lucky. He thinks a quick wash all over with crushed ice and rub down with a dead hedgehog toughens you up. I prefer to soak and get really WRINKLY. I will stop when I am 20 and hope I haven't got a skin like a tortoise by then.

BOOKS

My Father has a cartoon on his wall where a V. Worried-looking little man is sitting with his head in his hands in a massive library, and his wife is telling somebody 'He doesn't believe a single word he's read in the last ten years.' I wish I could graduate to this level of Worry. Sometimes the fact that I've only read about six out of all the trillions of books there are in the world is so Worrying it feels as if they're all piled on top of each other on my head.

I think it is V. Likely that if you read a lot of books by Clever and Sensitive People, you will be Cleverer and Sensitiver yourself.

For Teenage Worriers books come in three sorts:

1) Schoolbooks like *The Great Gatsby* or
Sense and Sensibility. These are about People In
Society.

2) Presents, like the 'Narnia' books and *Black
Beauty* which you read when you were 10. These
are about Animals In Society.

3) Books You Choose Yourself like *Eat Fudge
And Stay Slim* or *The Magic of Cartier Bresson*.
These are about Youthful Optimism.

I think Daniel has read everything in the world,
so he doesn't have the Pile Of Books On Head
Worry. It's not just Old Poets like Keats and Shelley
and Roger McGough, but Benjamin Zephaniah and
Maya Angelou because Daniel says education is
'Euro Centrick'. I will casually ask him what it
means one day when we are sharing a Post-Passion
marshmallow.

Benjy hates getting books for presents but that is
what everyone gives him because it's easier when
you've only remembered his birthday three minutes
before the party starts. You'd think in this day and
age there would be books about Thomasina the
Tank Engine with coaches called Charles and Cyril.
But no.

I do worry about all those children who live
in houses with no books. But there are limits.
We have books in all the DRAWERS in our house.
They could be distributed among the poor. I am
taking all my old Pony books (except *My Friend
Flicka* and *Jill's Gymkhana* and two or three

other Big Favourites) to the Bubonic Plague Relief
Jumble sale. I am also hanging on to the Famous Five
for Benjy.

> **TIP:** If people are talking about a book you
> haven't read, don't pretend you have, e.g. I droned
> on about the Rainbow Lorikeet when Hazel's
> dad mentioned *The History of Mr Polly*.
> If in doubt, keep stum.

Rover can be
v. Jealous
of ↓

BOYS

If you added up the amount of time I worried
about boys this year it would probably be about
three months 2 weeks and 6 days. This amazes
me when I think of how much Other Worrying
I seem to be able to fit in as well. I would like
to say that Art, Photography, GCSEs and
Caring for the Poor were more important to
me. But just when you're trying really hard to
understand world politics, you find yourself
thinking of the Levi 501 advertisement which
is, incidentally, the nearest thing we girls ever get
to see of SEXY images of boys in the much
vaunted MEDIA (groan, whinge). There are lots
of MAIN WORRIES about boys, but they can
be broken down by the Chubb method into two
main categories:

1) Will any boys like me?

2) What are boys really LIKE?

The answer to the first question is that some boy or other will at some time or other, probably like you. It is often the case however (sniff, blub Etck Etck) that the Boy who Likes You (BLY) is not the Boy You Like (BYL).

When dealing with BLY it is better to be honest but it can backfire. I told Brian after he kissed me that I had thought about it for a long time and decided I would prefer our relationship to be Platonic, but he looked up 'Plutonic' in the dictionary, which means 'volcanic fires'. The next time I saw him he looked like a bullfighter wearing a rabbit suit.

When dealing with BYL it is better to be cool until they turn into BLY. With Daniel, I have never spent more than four hours getting ready if I thought I might bump into him at Hazel's house or in the street. And I would never send him more than five or six Valentine cards even now. It is better not to be too pushy.

Also, it is good to try and avoid always AGREEING with BYL or he will think you're soft. I think I have almost stopped doing this now. I may even tell Daniel that I don't think e e cummings is the very best poet I've ever read and that Benjy knows more about writing English. But I will hide my Atomic Kitten album.

Now the second, more complicated question:

BLY and BYL: The Difference

WHAT ARE BOYS REALLY LIKE?

I swing helplessly between two Eureka-type L. Chubb theories. One is that they are actually ALIENS. (B.O.Y.Z. – Beings Outside Your Zone.) They know the language, they have convincing Earthling Suits (one head, two ears, Etck Etck) but they are NOT LIKE US and what's more they DON'T LIKE US. They moan about girls who

Translation:
***Oh, Hooray. Now I will be enabled to don this excellent
suiting and engage in meaningful discussions with all
those charming Earthlingettes***

won't Do It, and call the ones that do SLAG,
SCHOOL BICYCLE, Etck. They think TITS
is the funniest word on the planet. In their original
form they must all be Round, because they are
fascinated by BALLS of all descriptions, and
when they get a bit bigger, by WHEELS of all
descriptions, because they also like going very
fast on things (including Girls, says Sandra
Crevasse in the Upper Sixth, with a meaningfully
contemptuous shrug which I always pretend to
agree with).

Boyz: As their mothers see them

As my mother sees them

As they really are

L. Chubb's opposite theory is that BOYS are JUST LIKE US, after all, only with WILLIES. I have to say that, when you look at ants, or kangaroos, or dandelions or mountains, then boys are certainly MORE LIKE US than anything else.

WHY they behave so differently is a conundrum, to be sure. I think it's because they get treated differently from when they were tiny. I heard of an experiment where a lot of little BOY toddlers were dressed in PINK and little GIRL toddlers in BLUE, and left with a lot of unsuspecting minders. If a BLUE toddler fell over it was told to be a brave BOY and if a PINK toddler fell over it was given a cuddle (incy wincy). And it continues. 'Cow' and 'Mistress' are BAD. 'Bull' and 'Master' are NORMAL, Etck Etck.

I am determined to bring my children up completely equally and give them every opportunity to earn lots and lots of money. But if Mr Hesseltine (our headteacher) came to work in a twinset and pearls I would still laugh. Which shows that EQUALITY OF THE SEXES has not got far yet. The only powerful men you ever see in dresses are judges and priests.

TIP: It is worth remembering that, however worried you are about BOYZ, they are also worrying about YOU and think you're from Another Galaxy too. Also, there is, apparently, someone for everyone. Look at Mr and Mrs Pipe two doors up. He's 6' 7"

she's 4' 2". We call them Mr Pipe and his better
quarter. Also, if you really don't like boys at ALL,
there are always girls. It is getting fashionable
to be a lesbian these days.

BRAS

All over the nation there are girls with V. Flat
chests. What are they doing? They are buying
over-the-shoulder-boulder-holders, i.e. BRAS!
They are padded ones, uplift ones, strapless,
slinky, cheeky, modest, cross strap, backless,
plunge neck Etck Etck Etck. And not a single
one to fit me! To be honest, I want a padded
one. Aggy wants a restraining one, built like a
muzzle. The closest I've got to My Ideal is wearing
a one-piece swimsuit with built-in cups under
my clothes because it gave me a Natural-Looking
Figure (as the ads say) but it was a nightmare
going to the loo.

Madonna hasn't helped in all this. She might be
a positive role model for today's Young Woman in
that she has a Career and is V. Free about her
Sexuality Etck Etck Etck, but you also can't escape
the fact that she's heavily into LINGERIE, even if
she does wear it over a bloke's pin-stripe suit.

Hazel told me a friend of hers went into a shop
to buy a bra and a headscarf for her gran. She
mailed the headscarf with a card and in her room

that night went to try on the bra. But the headscarf was in the carrier bag, so the parcel to her gran contained the bra!

I KNOW that nipples are for feeding babies and not for Mere Male Gratification and that if they show through your T-shirt you shouldn't be embarrassed. This has not stopped me collecting a drawer full of bras of different sizes, all uncomfortable. I will burn them one day. This was apparently a symbol of Women's Liberation, though My Mother says they usually only smouldered a bit. I wish they smouldered on me, it might make Daniel Helpless With Longing (phew, cold shower, What A Scorcher, Etck).

TIP: Wear something really loose and Stop Worrying. I have achieved this resolution four times this year, but three of those days I had the flu and on the fourth I was on a Duke of Edinburgh Award Scheme, wearing three anoraks. Next year I am going to BAN BRAS from my LIFE.

NB. Cats do not suffer from bra, bosom, cleavage OR nipple worry.

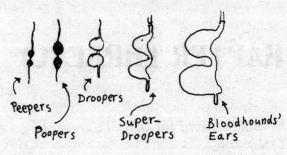

Peepers

Poopers

Droopers

Super-
Droopers

Bloodhounds'
Ears

PAH!

CHAPTER THREE (C)

(Over-the-moon except for school tomorrow, grue. READ ON.)

Yesterday was the best day of my life ever. Successfully covered the cold sore with six layers of HEY PRESTO vanishing cream and four layers of ERASERHED pancake goo which made it look a bit bumpy, but not too bad. Aggy and I were two hours early for the party and helped Hazel get her parents out of the house, and then rearranged the furniture, hid the jellies her mum had made and WAITED. Guess who came first??? (Swoon) His hair was the colour of wet sand at sunset . . . He danced with Hazel out of courtesy and Aggy out of pity (I was sorry I'd squeezed her into my lurex top to make her look glamorous because it just made her look like a liver sausage) and then he danced with me. I am over the moon. He brushed my hair with his lips! (Swooooooooon) I will never use a hairbrush again.

Hazel's parents came back at TEN, yawning. It broke the MOOD somewhat because her father overreacted about the CD player (all because it had a slice of ham in it. I thought they were famous for being unaffected by all Foreign Bodies, Fluffy Bits,

Acts of Dog, Etck) and her mother was unhappy about the jelly in the linen cupboard. Also they were not pleased about Hazel's brother and Zoe Carbuncle, who emerged from the spare room wearing expressions of what they call Mingled Emotions, like my cat Rover when caught in the fridge, or rather like she hopes she might look if she ever found anything in the fridge, groan, whinge.

Got back to blazing row about kitchen ceiling and unfinished novel. Apparently my father had got drunk and missed an appointment with a new agent. My mother says she can't paint for the worry. My father says if she likes painting so much he'll fix the ceiling and she can slap two coats of emulsion on it and do them both a favour, which didn't help. But do I care? No. I have danced with Romeo. I am on cloud zillion. I even kissed the sleeping pox-encrusted Benjy (aaah BLESS!) with my bare lips. I rinsed my mouth afterwards with KILLERZONE antiseptic, just to be on the safe side.

CARNIVORES

Creatures that stuff dead animals through holes in their heads. Many of them even claim to be human beings. I am planning to be a vegetarian.

CLEAVAGE

When Ashley was younger he used to stand very close to the telly and look downwards at the screen in a pathetic attempt to see down the dresses of the women in American Soaps, Etck. We had a student teacher wearing a floppy top once, and every time she leant forward all the Boys stood up, as if they were on opposite ends of a seesaw. This is the kind of Effect that Cleavage can have on Boys. Some Boys want to be seen with Girls dressed like this so their mates get all Envious and they get a reputation for being Evil Sex Machines From Hell. Some Boys want Girls to dress like this but call them

'In 50 years' time you will look like this'

Slags when they do. I think it's all to do with the
fact that Boys Are Babies For Ever, who want to
return to their Mothers and Abandon Themselves
between the Soft Orbs of the Beloved, Etck Etck.
No danger of anybody suffocating in my case boo
hoo, winge, curse.

If you must achieve this effect, the most useful
equipment is Big Buzooms as featured on Page
Three. If you don't have them, you can achieve
something similar with sticky tape and imagination
but the price of painkillers and your agonized
expression spoils it all. American girls used to do
exercises at SCHOOL to the chant of 'We Must,
we MUST, we must develop our BUST.' Americans
are really WEIRD.

Weeny Bop magazine says: '*INSTANT
CLEAVAGE – a touch of carefully applied blush
can work wonders! Dust loose face powder over
your chest, then brush a little blusher down the
centre of your cleavage for the illusion of added
depth.*' Ever tried getting blusher off a check
Viyella waistcoat? (Serves you right for wearing
one, Hah!) Anyway, I am improving. I have only
sent off for three bust-increasing creams this year
and one isometric spring developer, which I wasn't
strong enough to use.

TIP: Advice to Boyz: If you want a Girl to like you, try
and look into her eyes a bit when you're talking about
Eternal Lurve, rather than fixing your gaze at chest level.
This can make a Girl feel Unappreciated For Herself.

CLOTHES

The girls' mags go on about 'sexy dressing for
maximum effect'. Then they give you Tips which
are either:

1) DOC (Dressing On the Cheap) or
2) DGBU (Dead Glam But Unaffordable).

DOC tips go on about giving that old white
T-shirt sex appeal with Appliqué, fabric paints, Tie
'n' Dye, Etck and a whole lot of stuff that'll take
about a week to stick on and five mins to fall off.
Fabric paints cost more than a new T-shirt anyway.

They will also try to persuade you to turn the
T-shirt into a mini-skirt, turban, pair of socks, Etck
Etck. DO NOT SUCCUMB. Even if it all works,
you'll only end up looking like a kids' TV presenter
and if you really WANT a jumper with satin
bunnies on it you can get one from Mothercare.

DGBU tips are almost as bad, with flash-looking
girls called Karen and Amanda in cashmere two-
pieces with solid gold accessories mincing about on
penthouse balconies. You find these girls, who
complain of tough but thrilling lives in which Every
Day Is Different, are models on a thousand pounds
a minute and they're built like gazelles, rather than
giraffes like Moi. Yeeeeeech.

There's a lot of Krap about, believed by anyone
over 30, that girls today are not slaves to fashion
as they once were and that nowadays anything
goes. Well, we don't have to wear crinolines and

However you dress now . . .

in 50 years you will look like this . . .

bind our feet. But try telling that to someone
who has nagged her mother for two years for
stonewashed jeans, resorted to spending five hours
sitting in a bathful of boiling water in ordinary
jeans, rubbing them with PUMICE, wearing them
to dry (ker-*lammy*) then discovering stonewashes
are OUT and dead dark jeans are BACK, complete
with unopenable metal fly buttons. We still *souffre
pour être belle* and anyone who sez not is wrong
wrong wrong.

The V. Weird thing about clothes is that with all
the freedom we have today people still dress very
much like each other. Men almost never wear
dresses, or even doublet and hose, except when
they visit those ladies who advertise in telephone
boxes. In my Ideal World you should be able to

I'm all for sexual equality but . . .

wear ANYTHING. (Not that I would talk to anyone wearing an ANORAK. They give me Anoraksia Nervosa. Ha!) Then maybe Goths, Raggas, Beanies, Townies, Ravers and Casuals might get to SPEAK to each other. My ideal would be to be tipped gently out of bed and into a pre-selected assortment of tubes and flaps neatly washed and pressed by ROBOTS. No more rummaging under the bed fluff for that elusive SOCK.

Casual Sporty Outfit As worn in *Smirk* magazine

Awful Truth: it's NOT WHAT YOU WEAR BUT THE WAY THAT YOU WEAR IT. Hazel is a V. Good example of this. Put her in a binliner and a pair of bunny-rabbit slippers with a loo seat round her neck and she would still get into a Buck House Garden Party.

TIP: Get rid of all those zillions of cardigans (yeech), odd shoes, thermal vests and ACCESSORIES (money belts, earrings, bracelets, bags, Etck Etck) that you never use.

. . . and as worn by Teenage Worriers

It's not What you Wear it's the Way that you Wear It Dept:
Hazel in bin-liner, loo seat and Bunny-Rabbit slippers,
at St Mary's Academy Ball (moan, grr, envy)

Stop Worrying about what to wear. I wish I could.
Ask Yourself: Am I a vegetarian in leather *shoes*?
And have a little Worry.

COLD SORES

All last winter I was called Saddam at school because my cold sores are always just under my nose and when they dry up they look like a moustache. (Free brown paper bag available from the publishers when reading this section.) Before that I was called Pizza Face. I think Saddam was worse, but I hate pizzas so it's a close thing.

The Cold Sore is psychic. It appears JUST on the eve of an Important Date, or Party. Till now I've always used surgical spirit. Does the trick – but my Doc says it's medeeeval. Now there's a new Wonder Cream that starts with a z and zaps the little horrors in no time. NB: This is not recommended for other forms of Ye Herpes Virus such as the Private Bits one. Consult the Doc if you have this prob. Sorry.

CONTRACEPTIVES

The latest advice on these is always carry a pack of condoms. The question is, WHERE? Condoms themselves suffer from premature ejaculation (see SPERM) by leaping out of your pocket, money belt, purse, Etck when you are fumbling for your bus fare. They're trying now to make them look like fashion accessories so maybe soon we will be able to hang them from our ears.

As you know, I haven't actually DONE IT, but I have been carrying a pack for the last four years just in case. I am also probably the only person in the world who bought a pregnancy-testing kit (v. expensive) before I had started my periods.

And now, to my HORROR, I read that condoms have only a 70–80% success rate! So if you do it one hundred times you will have 30 babies! If you do it 25 times you will have 7½ babies! If you do it three times you will have just over one baby! It is obviously better to do it twice and then stop. Better still, always always use a contraceptive cream as well as a condom and MAKE SURE it's water-based as oily ones, even hand creams (Aaargh), can destroy the rubber.

There is a lot of fuss at the moment about whether teenagers should be given contraceptive advice without a long sermon from somebody crinkly about why it's better to wait till they're 30 or something. If you trust and like your doctor you should have no trouble over this, but otherwise go to a contraceptive advice centre. Don't let anybody put you on the pill without checking you're not pregnant first though. A friend of Hazel's recently had what is tactfully termed 'unprotected sex' (I used to think this meant sex without your parents watching) and the doctor immediately put her on the pill without checking. If she had been pregnant, this would have been V. Bad for the baby.

The Condom-as-Fashion-accessory

Other contraceptives include the Coil, a copper
squiggle that has to be put in by the doc, and the
Diaphragm, which is a rubber barrier you can
insert yourself. It's also called The Cap but don't
put it on your head because if your partner can
stop laughing enough to Do It you might get
pregnant. There is also The Pill, which you have
to remember to take every day; Creams which are
supposed to be used with Caps and condoms;
a new kind of Girls' Condom wot I don't understand properly; Vasectomy which is where the
boy has his tubes snipped and tied, but it's usually
for people who feel they either never want
children or have too many already and if you're
going out with a Boy like this maybe you should
reconsider your choice. Course, if you have
done it without using any contraception, or yr
boyfriend said you couldn't get preggers while
standing up, chewing gum etck, etck then get
EMERGENCY contraception (not very well named
as the 'morning after' pill). Can be taken up to
72 hours after having sex. Oh well, maybe you

And now, as part
of our Birth-Control
Programme: we present
Wednesday's weather
– sunny, with light
diaphragms

CAN bolt the door when the horse has bolted itself. But only if you're dead quick off the mark . . . You can get this from the chemist but there can be nasty side effects so only use as real last resort . . .

The most reliable contraceptive is Celibacy, which is Not Doing It. I am currently working on a Celibacy package that shows boys and girls just how much fun you can have without actually DOING IT. I am composing a letter to Mr Hesseltine (our headteacher) proposing that it be included in the National Curriculum.

TIP: Carry a pack of condoms and use them whenever necessary. Govt figures show Little Britain (once Great, sob, shame, decline, Etck) has a V. High rate of underage pregnancies with 170 schoolgirls getting pregnant every *Week*. (They must be keeping V. Quiet about it at Sluggs. I can only think of 3 in one whole year.)

COSMETICS

For us Socially Conscious Advanced Teenagers of today, aware of the Ecological Timebomb, there is now a vast range of guilt-free cosmetics NOT tested on Bunnies, Etck. But if they are not suffering, we all are.

The magazines have headlines like *18 Great*

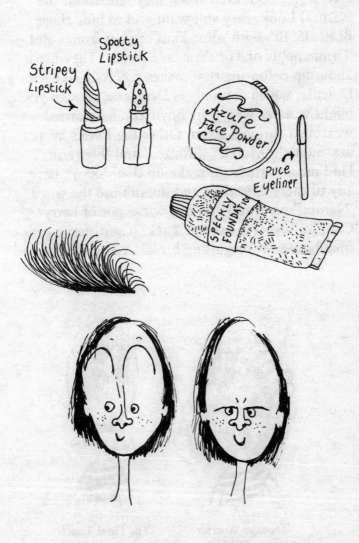

Stripey Lipstick

Spotty Lipstick

Azure Face Powder

Puce Eyeliner

SPECKLY FOUNDATION

Highbrow Eyebrows   **Lowbrow Eyebrows**

Ways to Update your Face for Winter (update your FACE???!!). But even when they talk about the Natural Look, they still want you to hide those BLEMISHES with some kind of glup from a pot. 'Dramatic' is one of their fave words. They use it about lip colouring that makes you look like Mrs Dracula, which certainly is Dramatic, though you might wonder why your Boyfriend has started wearing a surgical collar. Other Big Looks Words are 'Subtle', 'Muted', 'Bronzed' and 'Flattering'. Find me an article on make-up that doesn't have any of these adjectives and doesn't use the word 'Natural' once and you can win a pot of Letty Chubb's VAMP Cosmetic Pack. (Contents: green foundation for disguising broken veins, Purple and

Teenage Worrier
in L. Chubb's
Vamp make-up-kit

The Final Touch

Orange-stripe shimmer-look lipstick, Eyelashes made from genuine Tarantulas' legs, judge's wig, fake mole, and chic head-shaped paper bag with drawstring.)

CRICKET

This is Daniel's favourite game (swoon). He has vanilla-coloured flannels (gurgle) and a bat signed by some famous cricketer who takes Designer Drugs and gets thrown out of nightclubs for fondling the barman and punching the hostesses or whatever. I do not see why more girls do not indulge in this glorious sport of kings, since it involves no bone-crunching physical contact and is V. Soothing to listen to – clunk, thwap, rustle of cucumber sarnies, ripple of applause as ball rubbed on bowler's willy, Etck Etck. There is a danger you may be killed by the ball but we all have to go sometime.

CHAPTER FOUR (D)

*School (grue.) GCSEs are looming but maybe I
won't stay on for 'A' levels after all. I am going to
a desert island with a sand-haired man, to write
poetry. My Mother is whingeing about the kitchen
and the family finances. She is in despair that if
things don't look up I won't be able to take my 'A'
levels at St Winceyette's Academy or wherever. I
told her there were millions of people starving and
surely that was more important than a private
education!!!! But she burst into tears.*

*I think the final straw was Benjy asking for the
MEGAMAXI BANANA-RAY MIKRON
SUPERKILLER SPACEMOBILE for Christmas.
It costs £57.89 and it is only OCTOBER. She
cunningly directed Benjy to go and ask his father
for this little item, and the little pustule was
surprised to be told by a man reluctantly dragged
from the depths of the* Readers' Digest DIY Book
that the older generation was reading King Lear
*at his age and not rotting their brains with a lot
of cruddy old American Junk Culture. I asked,
as if I couldn't imagine the reason, why he'd
therefore shown so much interest in Kim Basinger's
scenes in* Batman *and he said how could we
waste time going on like this when the Govt*

*was postponing the election yet again to deny
the People the Equality that is their birthright?
He went out to the pub at this point, my mother
informing him that if he wanted to be equal
with most of the husbands she knew he might
consider providing for a few essentials for his
dependants.*

*I soar like a swallow above all this tawdry
rubbish. Daniel goes back to school next week and
we are going out TONIGHT.*

DANCING

Dances these days are V. Energetic and Jerky. They
all look like Aerobics Programmes. When Justin
Timberlake or Busted do them it looks OK but I
have the physical coordination of a pantomime
horse, and one where the front and back halves are
in Divorce Proceedings at that.

TIP: Don't try and do dances for V. Fit, properly wired-
up people unless you are blessed in this way yourself
or you will just look like something out of the *Muppet
Show*. Slink about V. Langwid instead and look as if
you save your Undulating Loins for much more
Interesting Things.

DANDRUFF

Dictionary def: 'Dead skin in small scales among the hair. Scurf.' My def: 'Dead skin in vast scaly lumps that pitter patter on yr plate, desk, lurve-object's nose, Etck.' V. Worrying.

Save your dandruff to delight your sibling with a home-made snowstorm

TIP: Wear light-coloured clothes. Hold head completely still at all times.
Don't comb hair in public without issuing megaphone warning and evacuating area, and don't scratch.

DANIEL

Dictionary def: 'Upright, judge, person of infallible wisdom.' How V.V.V. True (sigh).

DARK (FEAR OF)

Just because you like to sleep with the lights on does not mean you are a baby, it means that you have Separation Anxiety.

I have V. Bad Separation Anxiety. I do not like getting up in the morning. Nor do I like going to bed at night. I leave the house like a snail (o lucky snail that hath its house on its back)

Benjy by Day   **Benjy by Night**

and I dawdle on the way home, Etck. I do not like turning lights off because it means saying goodbye to the day. Also because it is Dark when they are off. Benjy is the only person who truly understands me.

DATING

Aaargh. Problems:
1) How to get a date
2) What to wear
3) Where to go
4) What to say
5) How far to go
6) How to get another date
7) How to avoid another date

1) How To Get A Date
Easy. Just ask. You will notice that boys ask girls out more often than girls ask boys out This is to do with CONDITIONING and should by now be regarded as Outdated Sexist Krap. The Object of Your Desire will say 'yes' or 'no'. However, it is worth remembering that some parents, especially GIRLS' parents (moan, whinge, grrrrr) are V. STRICT. So some girls (ie Moi) are only allowed out one or two nights a year and it might be worth persevering.

2) What To Wear

Get comfy, but if it's someone you really like, it is worth making an effort. This rules out anoraks, pac-a-macs, rain hats, mittens, shell suits and cycling shorts. I never spend more than three or four hours getting ready if I'm going to see Daniel and I make a big thing of looking like I haven't tried at all. It is An Art.

3) Where To Go

A little research is advisable. As a first date, I wouldn't like two tickets for a rugby final or the spider-house at the zoo, but to some these things would Set The Heart Aflame. As a rule don't spend a first date sharing a glass of Nerve Tonic with your parents.

4) What To Say

It is V. Touching, but boys and girls worry EQUALLY about what to say on a first date. Boys quite often try to get round this with stuff like 'If I said you had a cute little body would you hold it against me.' Another common mistake is to be too Kool. A few grunts might have been OK for James Dean or even Sylvester Stallone ('Is this my brain, or WHAT?') but you need the hair, the bones, the jeans, the car, the reputation and the dosh to get away with it.

Getting-to-know-you questions like 'Do you like string?' are V. Sweet but land you in a one-word-reply-situation. If you can't think of anything to

NB. Tip: To meet Opposite Sex, get a dog

say and you're not interested in what your date is saying then you aren't getting on.

5) How Far To Go

If you Do It on the First Date you may find the Boy Of Your Dreams tells his horrible mates and you get called School Bicycle (moan, whinge, not fair) while he gets treated as Superwilly, Lurve

Machine, Etck. I am composing a letter to the Govt
to change the rules on this as it is V. Unfair indeed.
Still, if anyone's going to get left Holding The Baba
it's you, and anyway you can get lots of fun without Doing It.

Boys are Prats about this and often think a Girl
can't get pregnant if the Boy is Drunk or Pulls Out
In Time, or the Girl is having a period, or they're
Doing It Standing Up. This is all Rubbish.

6) How To Get Another Date

Ask. If it has gone well, your date will reply
'Why, yes, I'd love to,' and maybe even Blush.
If it has gone badly they will say they feel they're
coming down with Beri Beri or that they're too
screwed up and horrible for a Nice Person Like
You. Try not to fight against these signals, it leads
to Heartache and Pining.

7) How To Avoid Another Date

If the date made you wish you had toured a
Stately Home instead, don't ask them out again.
If they ask YOU, say you're a bit busy and no
thank you.

If you stick to these 'dos' and 'don'ts' you
will find the Chubb method can work for you.
I confess I don't always stick to them myself.
I would like to dress My Way with Daniel
frinstance, but he likes sequinned mini-skirts and
15 denier tights and I can't bring myself to think
of him as a sexist creep because I am sure he will
grow out of it.

DENTIST

Go a lot because once you are 16 it costs a fortune. Dentists' waiting rooms are famous for copies of *Time* magazine and *Country Life* published when you still had your baby teeth. They play thrilling music like Simon and Garfunkel tapes and sink a smoking mineshaft in your precious fangs faster than you can say 'No, it's the one on the LEFT!' They still ask you such things as your opinion of *The Collapse of Communism* or *The Literary Significance of Eminem* while your mouth's full of vacuum cleaners and little silver trowels, so I hope they don't work out the State of the Universe from what their patients tell them.

DEVIL

V. Worrying in theory as the embodiment of all EVIL. Generally reckoned to look like Jack Nicholson in *Batman*, *Witches of Eastwick*, Etck but also have horns, cloven hoofs, Toasting Fork for roasting babies on, Etck Etck. I am still a bit suspicious of any of the teachers at Sluggs with esp. bushy hair or small feet, for this reason, and even got a bit Worried about

Benjy after seeing a video of *The Omen*, though
if Benjy is The Devil he's in V.V. Brilliant disguise.
I have been Worried about this since V. Young, and
used to ask babysitters to take their shoes off before
my parents went out, which everybody thought was
SWEET (they'd have smiled on other side of Fizz if
I'd been right, grrrr, what do they know).

DIETS

It is V. Worrying how many teenage girls are on
diets. Young girls go with their mums to FATTY-
WATCHERS, Etck, where they both get the weigh-
ing machine, pep talk, little gold stars and certifi-
cates. These orgs. also make loads of dosh out
of special diet meals, pleasure-free-chicken-salad-
in-an-easy-cook-pack, Etck Etck. A telly person
asked one of these girls' Mums what she hoped
for her daughter and she said `I hope she will
realize she has a weight problem and learn to
cope with it,' rather than hoping she might be an
astronaut/Lurve Goddess/turf accountant/physicist/
manicurist/human cannonball.

There are 50 zillion diets on sale each week at
any chemist or newsagent you pass. Let's face it, if
these diets worked, no one would be fat, would
they? Some people are just fat because they are.
But if you are really worried about it, then one

The Teenage Worrier who lost weight (but not fat)

good way is to eat three quarters of each meal instead of all of it.

> **TIP:** Worry a Lot. It works for me. NB: Must get a big stock of Plumpo in. And try to persuade Aggy to wear that nice vertical-striped tracksuit instead of her loominous pink culottes.

DIVORCE

V.V. Worrying. Everyone I know who still lives with two parents (an increasingly small majority) is V. Worried about it. Parents like to argue and this makes teenagers Depressed. Of course, teenagers like to get Depressed and this often makes parents Argue, so it cuts both ways. But parents also love to divorce and this makes teenagers more Depressed. Even though Aggy's Mum has now been with the postman for a year and a half, she and Aggy's father have not actually divorced. This gives Aggy a frail thread of hope on which to weave her dreams of a happy reunited family, roses round the door, Etck. But lots of people have only ever lived with one parent or even no parent and lots of my friends' parents never married anyway. I might as well admit that this included mine in actual fact; my father thought it was all Bourgwois Krap, Etck.

Are they splitting up because I'm depressed? Or am I depressed because they're splitting up?

Walt Disney's Happy Little Families of cutey bunnies Etck, or big snow-covered Daddies clutching dogs they've rescued from mad bears and watching Mother knit their paws back on by a crackling wood fire, tra-la-la, they're to blame for all this. Poor, honest, and TOGETHER! When we have children, Daniel and I will never argue in front of them. The main reason I am doing this book is to make loadsamoney so that my parents will not have to worry about bills, etck and will stop arguing. I would rather have them arguing than not around, I admit it, but I have met quite a few kids who were relieved when their parents split up because it meant the bread-knives stayed on the breadboard. And when they split up 'amicably' and everyone sees each other all the time it can be quite fun: Two houses to lose your homework in, and lots of Guilt so you get more presents.

TIP: If your parents split up it is not your fault. If one of them tries to stop the other from seeing you, get help. It is the pits to stop children from seeing a parent they want to see.

DRINK

As we know from pix on the News of cursing,
bandaged barstaff in Benidorm, Etck, Brit Yoof do
not deal with Drink as well as they might. Brit
Crinklies do not deal with it as well as they might
either, as I realized the morning I went to the loo to
find My Father asleep with his head in the bowl, or
in the magistrate's court when they read out My
Mother's advice to the policeman who arrested her
for driving drunk the wrong way up a one-way
street, and which is not repeatable in a Family
Book such as this.

This is the kind of example from the Older
Generation which confuses their Offspring. I
should say I do not have a problem with Drink.
I find the kind of beer Ashley likes tastes like
washing-up water, wine smells like the stuff My
Mother cleans her brushes in, and lager looks like
what you sometimes have to take to the doctor
in a little plastic jar. I did have two glasses of
whisky mac at a grown-ups' Christmas party once
and tried to introduce a vicar to a rubber plant,
but generally I do not find this a particularly great
Temptation.

Judging by my Friends, Boyz are more prone
to booze than Girls, because they think that
drinking too much, shouting, fighting, puking,
Etck is Macho. I suppose this means it is either a
Mating Ritual – in which case Boyz, beneath it

all, really want to mate with hippos, skunks and other similar species rather than Nice Things like Girls – or a Companionship Ritual in which a mark of respect is your friend's fish supper over your 501s.

TIP: Avoid getting drunk. Apart from making you prone to accidents, fights, Decisions You Regret, or just Prone, you miss all the Fun you might have had from talking, dancing, posing, snogging, Etck because you're incapable. Mineral waters and alcohol-free lagers now have big Attitude-type images while Ginger Beers, Lager Shandies, Etck are nerdish drinks and shld be avoided if you wish to Maintain Your Dignity.

DRUGS

Once you are over 18, nobody can stop you from buying a drink. This does not go for most drugs commonly discussed among the Yoof of Today, which are illegal – and therefore a major reason for being V. Careful of them in my opinion. My parents, who generally do not know whether it's Christmas or Easter, nevertheless get V. Wound Up on the subject of Drugs and keep imagining that my pic will one day appear in the *Sunday Sport* under the headline 'DRUGS MADE ME

SEX SLAVE TO 400 ACCOUNTANTS' Etck.
I once found an undergraduate pic of My Father
in a newspaper from the Sixties, sitting naked
in a field with a Big Daft Smile on his face,
accompanied by several Girls (also wearing
BDSs and nothing else), making daisy-chains.
The headline was 'DRUGS TURN CREAM INTO
CABBAGES'.

My Father and Mother don't pretend they never
smoked pot (neither do American presidents nor
archbishops these days) but say it was A Phase.
Yoof like taking stuff to pretend that whatever
they're having Fun doing will last for ever and
forget there are Awful Truths like Sluggs Comp.
Nobody I know thinks these things make you a
Junkie but because they're against the law and also
V. Expensive, L. Chubb Agony Aunts Ltd PLC
reckon it's better to lay off until you're A) old
enough to be legally responsible and don't lumber
your Poor Parents, B) rich enough not to be ruined
by the expenses.

Heavy Drugs are Lunacy. Don't touch Cocaine,
Heroin, Crack or anything Heavy. A boy Ashley
knew was a junkie – he turned from Norman
Normal into the saddest, most selfish and destruc-
tive person in the place and only straightened out
after he wrote off his Father's car and nearly killed
himself and somebody else.

NB The cheap stuff: Glue, solvents Etck
make you V. depressed and can KILL

DYING

DIVORCE, DRINK and DRUGS followed by Dying is not a V. Cheerful way to end this chapter so I bet we'll all be glad to get on to the 'E's before anything worse happens. But of course all Worries point to this one because it might happen to YOU or to Those You Love, so there isn't anything Worse.

I'm not so Worried about ME because I either won't know anything about it, or maybe get to

Rover does not worry about shuffling off this Mortal Coil

meet James Dean, Jesus, Etck which should be quite interesting. I do a lot of praying to avoid going somewhere Not V. Nice and meeting such as Stalin, Hannibal Lecter, Attila the Hun, Etck, but you can NEVER BE SURE.

But Worrying about it happening to Those I Love is my Meltdown Situation. I quite often shake members of my family if they're asleep and I'm not sure they're breathing. Benjy gave me a black eye once for doing this and my mother hit me with a hot-water bottle which burst.

Due to my Great Fear of the word that rhymes with 'breath' – I had to mutter my code-word for it ('Banana') throughout the school visit to *Hamlet* because Shakespeare is V. Keen on it – I have decided to mention this to my Doc, and hope she knows a cheap analyst.

TIP: If you find yourself saying 'take care' or 'mind the traffic' to people when they're just going to the bathroom, then an incy bit of Therapy might be the answer. Let me know how you get on. If your symptoms are not so severe, then this Worry is Quite Normal (as the Agony Aunts say) and indeed Universal. Viz Shakespeare, Etck.

('E's now, Wot A Relief. I must just tell you that last night was the best night I have ever had in my whole life. Daniel has sworn to write to me every day. We are wildly in Lurve. I must pour my soul into my Work and wait for Half Term . . .)

CHAPTER FIVE (EFG)

I cannot believe it. Daniel has not written. It is five weeks. I wrote a letter every day for five days after our glorious evening floating on the sea of Lurve, and now I have stopped.

My school work is suffering. My book is suffering. My skin is like the surface of the moon. It is half term next week and I will have no one to walk by the river with. No one to tell my hopes and dreams and fears.

I went riding with Hazel but it was dust and ashes. She is crazy about someone but won't give me ANY details. Aggy won the photography competition, for portraying the Human Spirit struggling for Redefinition in the World of the New Physics. Peryuke. It is terrible to think that people are making Artistic Judgements like these. Mine were serious pictures of tramps, winos and Granny Chubb movingly revealing that we are all ultimately just collapsing bags of snot and poo and stuff (except when transported on to the astral plane of lurve, like me and Daniel of course, or like I thought we were, swoon, Worry) and Aggy's were something anybody can do if they prat about in a darkroom for long enough.

I should be pleased for her of course, but where

oh where is the bright side of life? My mother has gone to her mother's for a week until the kitchen ceiling returns. I am babysitting for Benjy every night and cooking. At least Benjy and Rover love me, I think.

Last night I felt round the window pane to check no one had removed it during the day. I haven't done that since I was THIRTEEN and ... when I took my shoes off I put them together pointing away from the bed in case anyone was standing in them when I woke up.

V. Worried about a hedgehog I found last night, INERT outside kitchen door. Made it four bowls of bread and milk and put them round it so whichever way it is pointing it will see one of them and won't starve.

EARRINGS

My mother wouldn't let me get my ears pierced when I was 12 and since then I've been scared of AIDS. But just try and find a pair of clip-on earrings you can wear for more than half an hour without a local anaesthetic or that don't solve the pain problem by falling down the nearest drain. Also, try to find a clip-on pair that don't look as if they might have been chic in the Stone Age.

Daniel had a tiny gold elephant in one ear (CLASSY, sob). Wonder if the ear piercer sterilized the needle adequately, like suspending it for three months down an active volcano?

EJACULATION

This is a boy's orgasm (usually known as 'coming', which seems a pretty boring word for something they all think is the Best Thing In The World) and it's what boys are scared of getting a premature one of. Ashley said it happened the first time he held a girl's hand, but he didn't say what he held it against. Apparently the way to avoid it is to think of things like corrugated iron, Des O'Connor, Etck but as Ashley says you have to be careful or it can produce deflation. Really you need to think of anoraks, rice pudding, lino, Etck for a bit, then Britney Spears, Kylie, Beyoncé Etck for a bit (I reckon Boys are very rarely thinking about the person they're actually Doing It with) and then back to paperclips, cornflakes, telephone books and so on.

Mrs Pole down the road says the quicker they come the better as far as she's concerned, then she can read a Good Book. I bet Daniel could have gone all night and all day.

Now, perhaps, I shall never know.

ELECTROLYSIS

A method whereby little needles are used to remove unwanted hair more or less permanently. I would certainly use if it I got a moustache like Granny Chubb (as long as the needles were thoroughly sterilized in Active Volcanoes, Etck). In fact I have a few V. Teeny hairs on my chest that I am V. Worried about. One of the Agony Aunts I wrote to told me this is V.V. Common in girls and that electrolysis was the answer. I am currently snipping them and wonder just how V.V. Common it is.

ENVIRONMENT

I am V. Sympathetic about protecting the Environment, esp. since my own personal environment is

Always use both sides of a piece of paper

an Ecological Timebomb caused by unfinished DIY, baby brother's rubbish, blobs painted by Señora Picasso Chubb, Etck.

I have lectured Said Mother about her cosmetics, ALL of which are tested on animals, though she squirms a bit when you remind her that a little Rover or Horace has suffered so she can pretend she's got three less lines than you think. I was V. Shocked to find she puts right-on Ecosmirk labels OVER the labels on her Zap-A-Bunny beauty products and even puts napalm-style undegradable bleach into gentle, live-with-the-stains

Ecobleach bottles to fool you. Quel sham! Stung by exposure, she even said that when I did all the washing-up and remembered to clean the bath, Etck then I would have the right to choose the product!

She also puts all the rubbish in the same BIN, and doesn't bother to recycle the newspapers, saying it wastes more energy in petrol to take them to the dump than it saves in re-using them. All this goes to show that the adult race is unfit to govern and that we teenagers should take over NOW and set things to rights.

This is how it would work:

1) Traffic Congestion

Allow half the drivers to drive on Mons, Weds and Thurs and the other half on Tues, Fris, and Sats. Special dispensation for doctors, Etck. (And members of the Govt, like Moi will be by then.)

2) Accidents

All vehicles to look like fairground bumper cars, be made in V. Loominous colours and be V. Daft-looking to stop boys using them as willy extensions. Max speed of all vehicles except ambulances

to be 25mph (except also Govt vehicles, heh heh).
Motorways to be closed except to skateboarders
and cyclists (one lane open for Govt Rolls-Royces).
3) Trees

All citizens to plant one tree a year until the
Year 3000. (No trees with V. Big roots near Govt
property.)
4) Paper

All paper to be recycled (except Govt loo paper)
and a total ban on newspapers with more than one
supplement or half a page of sports coverage.

5) Hydro Carbons/Energy Consumption

One house per street to be turned into a communal fridge, ditto one washer and one dryer. (Exceptions made for hospitals and Govt members who need to do a lot of entertaining.)

6) Farming

All factory farming BANNED at once, offenders to be turned into pig-feed. Little chicks, lambs, Etck allowed complete freedom. (Govt property to be well fenced in.) Land to be given over

to useful crops, flowers, music festivals, Etck.

That's just a brief outline. There wld need to be some fine tuning.

So far, I am doing my bit by saving loo rolls for Horace and collecting empty drinks cans. It is hard to get into my bedroom for all the cans but I will get round to the recycling dept soon, or maybe I'll bin this lot and start again with something less bulky, like stamps.

EPITAPH

I Worry a lot about this because it's important to get your last message right. My favourite is:
   'Here lie I, Albert Onglebod
   Have mercy on my soul, Oh God
   As I would do if I were God
   And Thou wert Albert Onglebod.'
But I don't think you can do much with a name like mine. I quite fancy a simple message, like frinstance 'Not Working', which is what Benjy used to say when he saw a dead ant. I've got to decide, though, because you never know what might happen.

ERECTION

This pic has been censored

Boys Worry a lot about these. They are caused by blood thundering furiously into the little vessels inside the peacefully slumbering male willy on sight of the ridge caused by L. Chubb's left bra-strap under her jumper (or more likely Hazel's, grrr, whinge Not Fair), with the result that it becomes a proud Upstanding Organ ready to meet the responsibilities following the slipping of said bra-strap off the silken shoulder. When the Stone Age actress Mae West said things like 'A hard man is good to find' and 'Is that a gun in your pocket or are you just pleased to see me?' this is what she was on about.

The trouble with Erections is – apparently, ahem – they can leap up when you least want them at the sight of completely ordinary things like bra-straps, but get shy when faced with a Knickers-Off Situation and disappear. Ashley has told me about this, and says Girls have to be V. Nice if it happens and not chortle rude remarks or else the Boy may have lots more trouble with Erections unless suspended upside down from chandeliers dressed in binliners and beaten with rolled-up Kylie Minogue posters, Etck.

The trouble is, a Boy always thinks that he has actually got to DO IT or the Girl will tell her friends he's a wimp, and this increases his Worry about whether he CAN do it. And this in turn increases the likelihood of not being able to DO IT. Boys are V. Worried about their inability to PERFORM, which makes the whole thing sound like a circus. I do sympathize though. Girls do not have to get bits of themselves to go up and down like Meccano sets to have sex or even to have babies, so I suppose the responsibility of helping carry on the human race weighs on the willy (even if unconsciously since Boys always think they only wave these objects around For Fun).

For more on this see WILLIES. I know it's a childish word for PENIS and if we were proper grown-ups we would all go round talking like the people in *Casualty* but I don't want to be that kind of a grown-up any sooner than I absolutely have to. I know a five-year-old who says 'I'm going for a shit' because he's not supposed to use any coochy-coo words and I feel like holding his head down the pan. Also I do not like the way PENIS is an anagram of SNIPE and PINES. It sounds V. Scratchy.

EROGENOUS ZONES

Commonly held to be earlobes, lips, back of neck and any part of your body that turns you on when stroked by someone you like being stroked by. When I am in proximity to Daniel, I include my eyelids, thumbs and the bridge of my nose.

mmmmmmmm
mmmmmmmmm
mmmmmmmm
(ahem)

EXAMS

Exam results are Soooooooooooooo Worrying that I cannot Contemplate them without goose pimples

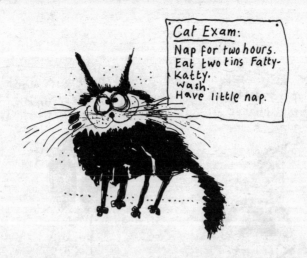

on my FEET! I am saving my biggest Worries about these until next year in case I spontaneously combust. Exam Terror is when you sit down to write and realize you have forgotten the alphabet. It affects a lot of Teenage Worriers and then they are consigned to the dustbin, scrap heap, Etck for ever.

Things have improved a bit since lots of the marking is done on the year's coursework (even though it is V. Easy to cheat and lots of pushy parents write all the essays and then get their incy darlings to copy them out, even introducing the odd forged SPELLING MISTAKE to make it look real, per-YUKE). I wish my parents cared enough to help like this but all they do is whinge about money and their work as if MY work wasn't going to be vital to the future infrastructure of the nation.

If I succumb to Exam Terror they will be V. Sorry they didn't cheat.

Exam Terror Takes Many Forms . . .

EXTINCTION

V. Worrying if happening to nice seals, graceful elephants, v. clever dolphins, etck. Less worrying in the case of wasps, midges, mosquitoes, stinging nettles. You may Worry about the Human Race becoming Extinct due to pollution, over-exposure to Dale Winton, Sun Blowing Up Etck.

Human Extinction is such a long-term Worry though, that even Moi has V. Long queue of other stuff to Worry about in between. See also ENVIRONMENT and THIRD WORLD DEBT.

FACE

'My face I don't mind it
For I am behind it.'

I don't know who wrote that but they must have
lived before mirrors, or in some frozen waste where
it's always dark.

If only it were true, and those blobs and holes
on the front of our heads were as we all wld like,
how happy a place would the world be. Aggy and I
reckon that if we added up the hours we spend
looking in mirrors we could have written six novels
or helped several thousand old ladies to cross the
road. This makes you ponder but it is V. Worrying
that it doesn't stop you doing it.

FAME

My favourite bathtime pastime is composing my speech about turning down the OBE because the Honours System is an outdated anackronism. Also, although I wld like to look EXACTLY like Julia Roberts I wld not like to be V.V. Famous like her and find zoom lenses poking out of the loo pan, reporters from the *Sun* under the bed, Etck.

I wld quite like to be Famous like Arty Lensman, Henri Cartier Bresson, who no one ever saw and who even covered his camera with black tape so he could pretend to be a lamppost, Etck. Or the Scribe Graham Greene who was dead sensible never to give interviews and now just dead of course (shame) so even less people see him. I wld like to be Miles Davis if he was still alive because then Daniel wld love me. I told Daniel what a great snooker player I thought he was. Anyway, snooker player or not, I am a white Anglo-Saxon non snooker-playing female, so he is not a good role model.

I guess I am aiming for a mix of Tarantino (Art), Steven Spielberg (Money), Spike Lee (Street Cred) and Madonna (Modesty).

The great thing about film directors is they get all the credit even though writers and actors and editors do all the hard work. Nobody knows the name of the woman who wrote *ET* for instance. Also, nobody knows what Directors look like, so they can still have baths, Etck in peace.

FEMINISM

If I don't get into film school I may go into genetic engineering to see if I can build a Hermaphrodite. If you could make enough of these and observe them for a couple of centuries you could get a good idea of how we might behave if we didn't know we had to be EITHER Boys OR Girls. It would be a bit of a slow experiment of course and we'd have to hand it on to our children who might have forgotten what they were doing it for by the end, but it might lend weight to the Return of Feminism.

Feminism is supposed to be boring in the 21st century but I have read My Mother's copy of *The*

Girls are Brill. How come we don't get top jobs,
big money Etck?

Female Eunuch by Germaine Greer and I think it is V. Interesting and Relevant. That old postcard about women doing two thirds of the world's work for one tenth of the world's money is still more or less true EVEN THOUGH as the National Curriculum highlights (ahem) we girls are better at everything as little Enfants. How come we get less money then? How come we get less houses, seats in parliament, Etck? Unfortunately at the moment many Girls still refuse to face this Crisis and spend most of their time talking about boys and ROMANCE whereas boys talk about football and the Universe and the best places to kick each other, all V. Good training to be Captains of Industry, Presidents, Etck. Perhaps I will chain myself to something as a Protest – maybe Daniel (ha!).

FIGURE

These are all the bits of you that aren't your face, and it is hard to say which is more Worrying. Three main shapes have been named by the teenymags – Pear, Egg Timer and Grapefruit. This leaves out mine, which is Banana. It is V. Hard to find articles on what to wear if you are my shape, though I always steer clear of yellow with a black stripe.

TIP: If a Pear, tutus and cycling shorts not recommended, ditto Grapefruit. If Egg Timer, wear large filthy sack and give the rest of us a break. If a Boy with no biceps, remember lots of girls have no bosoms, so you will get on V. Well with them and share many happy hours comparing props.

If a pear or a grapefruit, tutus and cycling shorts
are not recommended

FLYING

Aaaaaaaaaaaaargh!

Major Worry. I KNOW fewer people per square thousand, Etck actually die in aeroplanes, but even when I am V. Famous I am going to go by boat and train. Since they are now making such Amazing Breakthroughs in the Nature of Matter, Etck, I don't know why they don't apply this to transportation so you could Fax yourself to Majorca and just shoot straight out of a box on to the beach in your daringly cutaway one-piece. None of that hopping about behind a towel or anything, let alone Flying.

> **TIP:** Go by boat, train or bicycle. Even America can be reached by boat as long as you've got lots of time and disguise yourself as a banana (not difficult in the case of Moi), or you go on a millionaire's cruise.

FORESKIN

This is the little flap of skin that rings the tip of Boys' Willies. If you are Jewish or Muslim, it is usually cut off when you are a baby. Sometimes it has to be taken off when you're older due to infections, but this is V. Unlikely. Basil in Year 10 used to draw faces on his, but he had to see a Psychiatrist after he pinned a polaroid of one over the nameplate on the Head's door.

FRIENDS

V. Worrying if you don't have any. V. Worrying if you do. If you don't, you mope about Nobody Caring. If you do, you worry about their Problems as well as yours, plus why you saw your B.F. linking arms with your Worst Enemy in the High St. There are zillions of letters to Agony Aunts about this, viz: 'Sandra is my Best Friend but yesterday I found her in Bed with my Hamster. Now neither of them are speaking to me.'

I am V.V. Lucky to have two Really Good Friends who I know will never let me down (although I am v. keen to keep Hazel and Daniel apart, and Aggy is getting a wincy bit *depressing*) and for whom I wld go to the ends of the earth and back again, though not in a plane of course.

> **TIP:** Friendship is like LURVE. The more desperate you are for it, the harder it is to get. This is V. Unfair, but some of the Letty Chubb advice on Boys is useful here, viz: Stay Kool. Do your own thing. Etck.

GAMES

Ashley used to say he could hear my muscles creak when I lifted a spoonful of cornflakes. You may conclude from this that I am not ideal sporting

How could someone whose muscles creak when she lifts a spoonful of cornflakes be exptected to wield a TENNIS RACKET?

material. You would be right, but nevertheless I am no weed, not I.

Believe it or not, I was V.V.V. Good at football in Primary School, and when I saw *Bend It Like Beckham*, I thought I could stop Worrying about what I would Do With My Life when I grew up. I thought I might avoid some of the off-duty activities, viz: Fighting, Crying, Etck as practised by Gazza and the like, but I felt I could bring back to the Home Of The Game all the ball-wheedling artistry so shamefully lost to Italians, Brazilians, Africans, Etck.

But when I got to SLUGGS, HARDLY ANY GIRLS PLAYED. Because GIRLS are supposed to play netball!!!!!!!!!!!!!!

This is an OUTRAGE, and I am getting up a

Wot might have been (sigh)

petition so the next gen. of talented young females may not suffer as I have done. In compensation I have gone to the other extreme and developed a fiendish aptitude for chess. This is a Game where you have to be really clever and which doesn't rely on Luck at all, which in my case is just as well. All over the world Boys and Girls are terrorized by Games, because people say they're good for the body and the character. But I know some fantastic Bodies with terrible characters and vice versa, so I think you should be allowed to develop whichever one seems easier to you. Why can't Nature Rambles (with the partner of Your Choice heh! heh!) be a Game? Or Yoga? Or Dancing? Or just waving gently in the breeze? End Games terror now!

GAY

Lots of boys and girls worry about whether they are Gay or Lesbian although hardly anyone dares mention it until they have left school. My feelings about Daniel have led me to the almost certain conclusion that I am heterosexual. Adults worry a lot about this and sometimes I think that if they heard their daughter was a prostitute or a smash-and-grab raider or a drug addict they could grin and bear it but if she was a lesbian they'd both DROP DEAD WITH SHOCK.

It's no wonder we teenagers agonize over it in these circumstances. But it's easy for me to say Don't Worry, because I am not Gay (I think). If I was, I'd Worry about it a lot, because a lot of the boys at SLUGGS still use words like 'Poofter' which is dead old-fashioned, and if you don't want to go out with them their best insult is DIKE. If you are brave enough you might make a really dirty joke about how you'd rather put a finger in a dike than lay one on any part of them but it takes courage, which is what V. Worried people lack.

Desert Island Frisks: Could you be Gay? Imagine you are on a desert island with v. nice people of the same sex as you for ten years . . . If you do not do any nooky with them you are definitely heterosexual.

TIP: If you think you are Gay and that you can't talk about it and you are lonely there are now loads of helplines and info agencies as well as loads of people just like you.
See also LESBIAN.

GEOGRAPHY

Despite the EC we Brits are not too good at Geography as we still think we are a World Power and that we invented everything, and have to spend all our time helping foreigners to tie their shoelaces. No amount of Hindi nursery rhymes in infancy have changed this yet, although I see a raylet of hope for the generation after Benjy's, because we might actually be part of Europe properly by then and have learned how to speak French. I have been learning it since I was 11 and all I can say is 'Parlez-vous Anglais?' To which the expected answer is 'yes', so you don't need to speak any more French.

Brits keep laughing at Americans because they didn't know where Iraq was until they bombed it and think foreign countries are just places to shoot terrorists and open McDonald's in, but I don't see we've got any reason to be superior. I have only just discovered that you could fit all of Britain into California with room to spare.

GLANDS

As far as I can tell, glands are little bags hidden away around your body, containing all kinds of stuff vital to your Internal Balances, Appetites (phew) Etck. The ones not hidden away are Buzooms On Girls and Balls on Boys. Glands are V.V. Worrying as they affect everything and can make you Fat, Thin, Hungry, Depressed, Manic, Etck Etck. So before considering yourself Mad and asking to see a Psychiatrist it's never a bad idea to have your Glands checked out by a Gland Doctor (this is not a Chinese person referring to the Royal Physician, ha!) and come to think of it I reckon I have glandular fever at the moment because my neck is swollen and I am V. Tired.

GLOVES

Occasionally you will see a lone glove stuck on a railing, but it is never YOUR glove. Is a glove fetishist cramming them into albums? If you find a blue woolly magic glove (the stretchy kind), a pink fingerless one, a red satin one or a big leather one that I borrowed off my Dad in the last week or two, could you post them to me, please, care of the publisher? Ta.

GOD

It has been V. Unfashionable to believe in God for some time, but even in Russia when it was not allowed lots of people went on doing it. It turns out that lots of people do believe in some kind of god but they don't like to say so – a bit like being gay. Also, churches are only ever any fun at Christmas when you get carols and trees, etck and they are never open any more if you just want to pop in (stained-glass windows even have mesh in front now, which shows you what a Terrible World we live in). Catholics and Greek Orthodox churches are great for people into fashion accessories because they go in for a lot of ornaments,

jewellery, Etck and West Indian churches attract the best hats.

I hedge my bets. I say a lot of prayers, like most superstitious people, and hope someone might be tuning in to some of them.

Flo in Year 13 refuses even to say 'Oh my God!' She always says 'Oh My Goddess.'

But the really Worrying thing about religion is that it makes you wonder why you are here, where you are going, Etck. Most adults seem remarkably unconcerned about it all whereas I think about it nearly as much as Clothes and Sex. I have tried to ask my parents what they think about but they say Worrying about these things is a luxury for people with time on their hands. Probably hermits, Cardboard City-dwellers and aristos on private incomes are thinking about it a lot, which will make the Chosen People a pretty mixed bunch.

GRAMMAR

Apo'strophe Catas'trophe?

This is the thing what everyone moans about teenagers not being taught any more (this is a Grammar Joke, ha!). If you mention English grammar to my father he hits the roof and bangs on about apostrophes because he can't bear the way greengrocers put up signs for

TOMATOE'S, Etck. If you do not know this is wrong, you're just the kind of person he's on about.

GRANDPARENTS

I only have two left and I worry a lot about one of them. Grandma Chubb knits terrible jumpers, tries to brush my hair for me (CRINGE), still sends me white ankle socks (double cringe), still thinks the TV is the Devil's work, still gives Boys bigger portions of food than Girls, still gets upset if I don't wear a dress on Christmas Day . . . and yet. And yet. Granny Chubb still sends me teddies (YES! I LIKE THEM!), still cooks me hot breakfasts if I stay over, still listens to everything and is never shocked except by appearances. What really Worries me about Granny Chubb is how much I'll miss her when she quits this Mortal Coil, whatever that means. I cry just thinking about it.

I admit I do not worry to the same extent about Granny Gosling, whose speeches about the State of the Nation make Hitler sound like Bob Geldof.

TIP: You might as well be nice to your Grandparents because if you are my age they probably won't be here for much longer (sob). Not only that, if encouraged they come out with V. Interesting stories about the past (this is Oral History and often much more exciting than a lot of what you get in books) and can tell you what it was like to have to live for weeks at a time on a plateful of dried worms Etck.

CHAPTER SIX (HI)

*Hedgehog turned out to be Red Herring. Well,
turned out to be a scrubbing brush actually. Now I
need my eyes testing as if I don't have enough to
Worry about.*

*My mother has returned with six enormous
canvases covered in scarlet and purple blobs. The
kitchen ceiling is almost back to normal and my
father has relented over the emulsion and had a
Good Meeting with his Agent. If my father can
only finish the book, the agent reckons the success
of Moving On still counts for something and my
father should be able to say goodbye to DIY
articles until all his children are Nobel Prizewinners
themselves.*

*My mother is very cheered by this. The agent
goes on about an American writer who spent
twenty years living off the proceeds of not finishing
a Great Novel so even if my father doesn't write
it there's some hope. It's a bit of a nerve say I,
when you think that Great Writers like Camus
banged out millions of novels of Human Destiny
and he was still forced to play in goal for Algiers.
But on second thoughts it may be just as well,
because my father has spilled some emulsion over
his word processor during his recent energetic*

*burst of nest-restoring and everything he tries
to write on it comes out in Greek letters now.
He may of course be able to fake a hitherto
undiscovered classic of the Ancient World and
spend the rest of his life with his feet on a desk
at Oxbridge. Ha!*

*I sometimes Worry because Father keeps his
Great Novel a Big Secret. I did once sneak a look
at the screen while he was out of the room and it
said 'THAT DARING YOUNG GIRL ON THE
FLYING TRAPEZE' about fifty times so I'm not
sure it's progressing as well as it should. I think he
hides the rest of it somewhere but I don't know
where.*

*Sometimes I Worry that my father may be a Dr
Jekyll and Mr Hyde, a decent crinkly bloke most of
the time, and a hairy loony who eats ferrets when
there's a full moon. My innocent mother has gone
out for lots of sloppy romantic dinners with him
since the agent cheered him up, but this only serves
to increase my sense of isolation.*

*This got worse when I danced with Brian at a
party on Sat and pretended he had sand-coloured
hair. But when he tried to kiss me I realized that
My Soul is On Ice. He apologized for cutting my
nose with his specs, however. Hazel keeps going
away for weekends and WON'T talk to me.*

*Hendon Snap said Aggy had 'Genius'. So much
for the opinions of our leading photographers. But
it hasn't made her happy. Her mother sent her a
postcard of a London Bus from Dominica, where*

she and her postman have sent themselves for an Autumn break.

Rover and Benjy both have tonsillitis which means the house is strangely QUIET. I try to talk to Horace but he just goes round and round. I am worried about my nose. It is looking v. bumpy. To comfort myself with the prospect of massive book sales, I will continue with:

HABITS

I turn lights on and off twice (I've got a thing about even numbers), always leave the bathroom before the loo has stopped flushing, never let the water run out of the bath before I've got out, try to avoid cracks in the pavement (V. Exhausting and induces odd, frog-like gait), hum in a low, bee-like fashion when I'm nervous (this is because Granny Chubb went to *The King and I* 36 times and told me when in trouble to Whistle a Happy Tune), bite my nails, twist my fringe round my fingers and, er, sometimes . . . feel round the edge of the window pane before going to bed just in case a Hooded Loony has removed it with a glass cutter.

I always pretend nobody else notices these things, but I fear they might. Benjy has even loudly enquired 'What you doin'?' in front of guests when I'm on my knees on the floor because when I drop

hmmm mmm
mmm (worry)
hmmm
mmm hmmm

Fringe
twisting

Checking
for Lucky
Rabbit's foot

Avoiding
cracks
in pavement

Sadly, treading
in dog poo as
result of pavement-
crack-avoidance

Moi, displaying small amount of rich panoply of HABITZ

something I always have to touch the ground twice when I pick it up. I think if I didn't have these habits I would be a lot more Worried than I am, because they kind of *diffuse* the Worry, but I am still aiming to stop at the rate of one a year from now on.

What's unfair is that some habits are thought to be signs of Madness and other perfectly disgusting

Nose Pickers of the UK

and offensive ones are seen as part of Life's Rich
Pattern. For instance Nose Picking, which Mrs
Tangent, the Maths teacher, goes on doing even
though we leave a false nose on her desk with a
Kleenex stuffed in it; Bum Pinching, which Jeff
Strode, the PE teacher, does when you go over
the vaulting horse (and he picks his EARS too,
sometimes at the same time). Mr Hesseltine,
the Head, clears his throat with a noise like an
alligator gargling in cement whenever he's about
to make an important announcement (eg 'The
whole school – yerk, screuk, crughhhh – will be

subject to the severest – screeeerch kyuk splut goo
– discipline unless the culprit owns up within ten
seconds').

Therefore, although my own habits (only the tip
of which iceberg I have listed) are fairly inoffensive
as yet, I feel I'm right to try to curb them before
they become like any of the above.

**TIP: If you have a really unpleasant habit like gobbing
in the street or picking your spots in public, try Letty
Chubb's Aversion Therapy. Do it for an hour in front of
a mirror. If this doesn't work seek medical advice.**

HAIR

A quick comb through the pages of *TeenyBop,
Smirk, Tru-Luv* and other rags offers a feast of

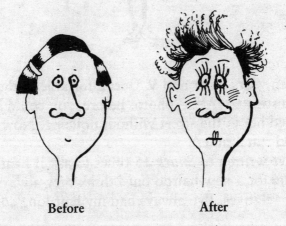

Before   After

Wig Worries. Perfectly pleasant-looking Yoof are subjected to endless Before and After treatments. *'We took advantage of Shirley's oval face to create a style that lifted her forehead (yeech), emphasized her cheekbones and minimized her strong nose and chin.'* Poor Shirley ends up looking

Afros are bound to be back in style soon

fifteen years older and V. Uncomfortable in the sophisticated 'After' photo. Before, you could have passed her in the street without noticing. Now you'd run a mile.

I've written to *Smirk* 15 times to ask if I can model for a new hairdo but I think they always use their relatives. I've always had my hair long so it

covers my neck. If it was short I'd look like a
giraffe with a vole's head.

Because of being called Scarlett, I put henna
on my hair last year. This is like boiling up a buck-
et of horse droppings, plastering it all over your
head and wearing it under tinfoil for three hours.
Then you spend the next three hours
scouring the bath, chucking out the towels and
sandpapering the remnants off the cork tiles
and your hands, so it's a day's work really, though
the effect is quite shiny. The hairdresser told
me it covers the hair with a sort of film and is not
half as healthy as it's cracked up to be.

Aggy is distraught that Afros are out of
fashion since that's all her hair will do, naturally.
Hazel of course has a tawny mane, a silken
waterfall, a sheaf of corn glowing in the setting
sun. She puts it up, down, curls it, braids it,

Hairdos: As worn in *Smirk*

The same hairdos as worn by Teenage Worriers

plaits it, buns it, corkscrews and beribbons it
and it remains a silken waterfall, sheaf of corn,
Etck Etck. Yeeeech.

But I dream of hair the colour of wet sand . . .

HEALTH

Basically the average Yoof (ie Moi) is more
concerned about *looking* healthy than actually
being healthy. Viz: endless droning in *Smirk* about
shining hair, dewy eyes, pearly teeth, glowing skin
and how to create them out of nothing in the
average underexercised, pasty adolescent slob.

I look forward to the day when you can hook
yourself up to your home computer and get an
instant medical check without all that Worry and
Disappointment of trying to convince a doctor
you're ill. Mind you, if the hospitals go on like this
they'll probably fax you instructions on how to do
a heart by-pass on your dad with the bread-knife,

My mother stuffs us with vits and mins . . . But do they work?

Me and Aggy having a little Worry about Health

or take your own appendix out with a tin opener.

My mother's latest thing is to dose us with vitamins and minerals (easier than bothering to cook) and leaving the windows open when she smokes (ie. all the time) so that we freeze.

> **TIP:** See your GP if you're Worried about anything. Dictionaries of Symptoms don't exactly stop you Worrying (eg most headaches could be meningitis and coughs are all terminal) but with the good advice of a friendly doctor you should be able to fit a little pleasure between the Worries. I can, of course, see that doctors have a hard time, constantly plagued for attention by millions of wimps with colds, and I do regret complaining of a tumour on my foot when in fact my shoes were three sizes too small.

HETEROSEXUALS

Have you ever wondered why no one worries that they might be a heterosexual? Not even me??????

HISTORY

Everything that used to happen. Still being made. Definitely the world's most enduring product and V. Hard to understand. We had a brilliant

swash →

buckle →

Moi: Studying Empathy in a Historical Context

History teacher in Year 8 who taught 'Empathy'. We all had to try very hard to be Roundheads one week and Cavaliers the next. Apart from the Boys thinking it was V. Funny to pretend they thought she meant Vauxhall Cavaliers and thus charging around going vroom vroom, it was

Tricky because from the Yoof point of view
Cavaliers had a lot more going for them – they
dressed better, had more dosh, nicer houses,
horses, hairstyles, Etck. However, thanks to
the Roundheads, we now have The Vote, and
anyone can go around telling stories of who the
Queen's relatives are sleeping with without fear
of execution, imprisonment in the Tower, Etck.
This seems only fair, since anyone can tell stories
about who I'm sleeping with, or they could if
I was.

HOROSCOPES

A complete and total utter rip-off. It would be
good if they said V. Definite things eg 'On Sunday
you will have a near fatal accident with an electric
toaster but on Monday you won't be so lucky.'
But it is all stuff that starts with a Downer (ie
looks, job, romance all going down The Pan) but
ends saying Beneficial Influences In Sight when
Moon conjuncts Uranus, etck. This keeps you
ever hopeful. It is no fun also if you are Taurus.
'Bore us with Taurus' should be the motto for my
sign: earthy, plodding, thick neck, love of gardens,
v. easygoing except when roused, all v. untrue
of me. But there have been lots of loony but
dramatic and V. Intellectual artistick Taureans eg

Karl Marx, Oliver Cromwell (to whom we owe
The Vote, pix of Queen's relatives Doing it, Etck
see above), Sigmund Freud, Michelangelo (the
artist, not the Turtle), William Shakespeare. All of
whom are much more like me (ahem). Daniel
is Sagittarius which is V. Fiery, free-spirited
(blush) but although often gets off with Taurus,
unfortunately tends to leave them for Aries.
This is V. Worrying, not that I believe any of it.
See ZODIAC.

HOSTAGES

I sometimes Worry that if I were taken hostage
for a ransom my parents would only snap
into action by renting out my room, as Woody
Allen once wrote. People are sometimes taken
hostage by terrorist groups and at time of
writing this situation is getting worse, and it
makes a Worrier like me think twice about
travelling outside the radius covered by my
bus pass. I have warned Benjy about this
and now he Worries about visiting Grandma
Gosling in Edinburgh. I don't think the Scots are
feeling that bad about us English persons now
they've got their own parliament. But you can
never tell.

HOUSING

When I was at Honeycombe Primary School, nearly all my friends lived in houses. They also had puffy little party frocks and strapped patent-leather shoes. Now, no one except Hazel and Daniel seems to have a house, they all live in blocks of flats where the lifts don't work and kids set fire to the dustbins. Brian is in something called Short-Life Housing which means the rain comes in everywhere and the loo never works and it therefore shortens your life. This is because the Middle Classes are vanishing from Inner London.

The Streets of London Are Paved with Gold

The Govt has cleared up Cardboard City, a shanty town of cardboard boxes that was V. Upsetting for all the people who wanted to see Great Artists portray Poverty, Deprivation Etck at the South Bank Arts and Leesure complex but not the Real Thing. But the dossers are just more spread about now. There's zillions of teenagers wandering the capital's streets and shacking up in a pile of newspapers. Even so, my father refuses to distribute his piles of newspapers to the poor because he needs them for 'research'. How Socialist is that?!

IDEAS

'The Best lack all conviction. The worst are full of passionate intensity.'
Ever since Ashley told me that quote from ye great Irish poet Yeast, I have been V. Worried about my Passionate Intensity. He has a point, since lots of wars were started by loony crusaders who had an IDEA. On the other hand, Humanity has not Got Where It Is Today by people sitting around in mud picking fleas out of their wigs.

I am also V. Worried that my ideas might run out. I'm sure that by the time I really need them ie when I have to earn a living, which could be next YEAR (yeeeeech) they'll all have run into the sand, as eventually we will ourselves (groan, sigh, make sign of cross, look mystified into Great Beyond, Etck).

The fact is, teenagers have about a million ideas a week and small kids have about a trillion. If we could stick electrodes on babies' little balding heads and translate the messages into Adultspeak, world poverty would doubtless end at a stroke. Benjy's latest is a device for retrieving marbles from the middle of three-lane highways without risking life and limbs. Letty Chubb's solution: TEENAGE THINK TANKS, so that Society can benefit from the free-flowing Brilliance and Energy of Yoof in all its glory before the idealistic petals droop, Etck.

I am worried my Ideas might run out

**If we could stick electrodes on babies' little balding heads
and translate the messages into Adultspeak . . .
world poverty would end at a stroke
(and I would get V. Rich)**

When people talk about Ideas, they can of
course mean anything from a new way to get
chewing gum out of the carpet to the best way
of organizing the World for maximum Peace,
Harmony, Justice, Etck. I think the latter are
most Interesting, though carpet and chewing
gum manufacturers might disagree. The main
ideas in the Peace/Harmony/Justice field are:

Just a sprinkling of the IDEAZ that might be generated by the T.T.T. (Teenage Think Tank)

1) If everyone takes care of themselves and the Govt leaves them alone, everything will find its proper level, adequate supplies of everything necessary will be available at sensible prices, and All Will Be Much Better.
2) If everyone takes care of each other, shares everything, and talks about problems, and the People's Govt replaces the Rich and Powerful, All Will Be Much Better and adequate supplies of everything will be available at sensible prices.

PS. If you have any v. good ideas for saving the world, uncovering the meaning of life, how to be happy, etck, send them to me care of the publisher and I'll see if I can get the ball rolling. You'll get a small royalty if any of them make money – I mean add to the welfare of humankind (heh heh). See also POLITICS.

IDOLS

Mine are Marilyn Monroe and James Dean. This is, according to famed cultural pundit Prof. Zeitgeist, a prime example of 'cultural necrophilia', ie we all love people who are Dead, which is V.V. Worrying. An idol is anyone you want to be like, and I admit it probably

Benjy has an idol . . .

seems weird to prefer Marilyn to Britney. But anybody who'd rather be Orlando Bloom than James Dean is Mad, a Fuel, Etck.

ILLITERACY

A Mager Crysis. Ha! V. Worrying to my Mum, who thinks Benjy will never learn to read four-letter words (not that she lets him say any).

Also V. Worrying to me as it means less people will buy my book. Which is why I've put in so many pictures.

INTERCOURSE

See SEX. Don't turn to it yet, you'll go blind.

CHAPTER SEVEN (JKL)

*A letter from Daniel! (Extracts only due to length
of DH's outpouring of soul.)*

> '*Dear Scarlett,*
>   *I am sorry not to have heard from you after
> those first wonderful letters and I imagine that I
> must consign the memory of our walk by the river
> to the dustbin of my dreams. It would have been
> kinder if you had replied to my earlier letter saying
> let us just be friends or some other euphemism.*
>   *At least then I could try to gather up the
> tattered fragments of my life and try to find a
> path through the endless desolate wasteland that
> now stretches interminably before me.*
> *Yours sadly,*
> *Daniel.*'

*JOY! EXQUISITE JOY! Confusion! Sadness!
But where was the missing letter??*
   Benjy?!!!
   *Dashed off 25 page letter to D., ransacked
Benjy's bedroom. He croaked pitifully that he had
nothing to hide and after going through all his
drawers, toy boxes and clothes I concluded that
wasn't true, but at least he didn't have the letter.*

*(Found in Benjy's yukky premises: 9 conkers
(3 split), 14 marbles, 1 part-used packet Big Boy
extra-sensitive condoms marked WORTA BOMS,
5 euros (fraudulent payment for Benjy's fruitgums),
4 Mega Zygon bubblegum cards, Ball of wool,
One-legged Batman, Christmas Snowstorm (leaking),
3 buckets of Lego, Blob of fluff held together with
chewing gum.)*

I think it's disgusting my mother doesn't take better
care of my baby brother's things. But where was
the letter? HORACE!! Looked just like shredded
loo rolls in his cage. How could I be SURE?

To cut a short story long, I finally found it in
the back of my Father's desk drawer along with
a dirty magazine, six final demands on various
essential household items (including the HP on his
Encyclopaedias) and bits of The Great Novel. In
my Great Wrath over the letter I have taken an
Eye for an Eye and hidden My Father's Artistic
Ravings. I am surprised to find after the first few
pages that it is about a family man who runs away
to build a log cabin in Wales and lives by himself
with a dog catching fish (the man, not the dog). It
was all a bit buttock-clenching to read actually, but
things could have been worse. He might have run
away to become an Evil Sex Machine From Hell.

I confronted My Father about the Letter and he
pretended he hadn't noticed it was for me. I told
him he was a possessive megalo-maniac who didn't
want his daughter to grow up.

Went to Aggy's. She was coming round to see

ME, in TEARS because her father has moved a GIRLFRIEND in 'to help with the kids'. We locked ourselves in my room and I felt so sorry for her and so happy about Daniel (swooooon) that it took my mind off the animated discussion my parents were conducting about the bills.

Benjy has started to worry about the kitchen floor. He says he can see FACES in it. My father said he would change it, but my mother said she would leave home. We are a v. neurotic family.

Showed DH's letter to Aggy, which made her cry harder. It went on about the Majestic Tumult of my hair, the Fawn-like nervous grace of my Bod, Priceless Jewels of my Eyes, Etck Etck, which all made me feel a bit Wobbly, including in the places DH fortunately didn't mention.

The more I thought about it the more I wanted to Kill My Father, but I will let him off just this once. I am rather touched by him wanting to live in a Hut Away From It All. It's better than living Away From It All whilst pretending to be living with us, which is what he actually does.

I will attempt to get briefly Away From It All by getting on with JAYZ.

JOBS

Aaaaaaaaargh. Yeeeeeech. 'Wot's a job, Dad?' 'Don't know, son, ask yer grandfather.' Etck, Etck.

The Careers Advisory Officer at Sluggs asked
if I had thought of a career manufacturing
artificial limbs. I told her about my plans to
be a film director. When she stopped coughing
and spluttering she muttered on about the
lack of openings and the decline of the Brit
film industry.

I will say this for my mother, she is v.
encouraging about my ambitions, even if it is
always accompanied by speeches to the effect
that she only wished SHE had had the confidence
to think of being a film director when SHE was
my age, whinge moan cast-eyes-heavenward-at-
opportunities-missed Etck.

Also, there is the basic diff. between JOBS

JOBZ: What is the future for Brit Yoof?

which you do for MONEY NOW and CAREERS which you do for long-term satisfaction and future prospects (ie making loadsa money – I mean fulfilling your Spiritual Longings and Improving the World, ahem).

> **TIP:** Make long lists of OPTIONS. Check
> out which exams you need. You will get masses
> of conflicting advice on this, so take an average.
> Do not get fobbed off with V. Badly paid Work
> Experience Schemes unless you think they are
> really teaching you something about what you
> want to do – V. Unlikely but you never know –
> or maybe helping old people which is V.V.
> Useful and gives added glow of smugness which is
> good for the skin-tone. Campaign, write to
> your MP, Protest, dance naked in streets for
> TEENAGE THINK TANKS (see IDEAS, above)
> which should be v. highly paid and v. cushy . . .
> ahem, v. useful to society.

JUSTICE

When you have already been in prison for a decade or so for something you didn't do you may eventually get out and everyone says Brit Justice is a Wonderful Thing and knows how to Right Wrongs, Etck. The ex-prisoners don't feel quite the same about it.

You have to Worry about Justice a lot – at home, at school, at work, everywhere. It means people getting their fair share of the credit and dosh for something good they've done, or their fair share of the aggravation for something nasty or stupid they've done, and not being blamed for something that wasn't their fault.

The police, being at the Sharp End (ie on the streets, Scene of the Crime, etck), get a lot more flak than lawyers and judges which is V. Unfair, since it is lawyers, Etck who actually present all the evidence and argue it all and the best talker wins. If the best talker won in our house, Benjy would be sleeping in the loo and eating potato peelings. He shtill lithps.

> **TIP:** If in trouble with the law, do not try to be funny. My own Father, who was breathalysed a few years ago, said 'I admit I've been driving but I'm perfectly fit to drink.' This did Not Go Down Well. He might have done better if he hadn't been wearing a Free the Tottenham Three T-shirt. Whether black, white, girl, boy, gay, lesbian or indifferent, speak as politely as possible and call the policeman 'Officer', even if he looks like Al Capone. If you need a character witness it is best to go for a vicar or a teacher than the V. Nice drunk you befriended under the flyover, who lives in a cardboard box.

NB. A recent survey revealed (as they say in the papers my Father refuses to recycle): Only 10% of

The Judge knocks on Heaven's Door

Britain's 107 judges are women. Of the High Court Judges, only SEVEN are women. And how many are from ethnic minorities?

KEYS

Us Yoof are always losing Keys, because we live such an active Lifestyle full of Surprises, like seeing the Boy/Girl of your Dreams just as you're opening your front door and forgetting all else, including the fact that your key is still in the lock.

TIP: If you lose your keys, change the locks to avoid outbreaks of intruder worry.

KILLING

I am V. Worried to be a member of the human species, which is one of the very few creatures that kills its own kind. A couple of brands of ants and monkeys also do it but generally animals are v. peaceful.

Most murders are done by someone who knows you well. If you think about this too much you will get V. Worried – plus avoiding everyone who knows you well will make people think you are

Most murders are done by someone who knows you well

V. Strange and may lead to loneliness. Domestic murder (which is the cuddly name police give it) is most common among husbands and wives; usually the man murders the woman. A good rule to avoid getting in this situation is, if a boy is ever violent to you, never see him ever again. I was V. Worried to discover about domestic murder as I thought if I stayed in all the time with a lot of locks on the house I would be safe. You can't win.

KISSING

It gives you some idea of what kind of book you're dealing with here, when Kissing follows right on after Killing. Anyway, they say that the one memory that age does not dim is your First Kiss. (I'm not sure of this. Mine was 14 months and six days ago in the back row of the Ritzy at a V.V. Scary film.) It was with Simon – tall, dark and handsome and a Boy for whom I had extremely strong URGES. These did not altogether survive the fact that he didn't take his gloves and scarf off. He also told all his mates I was a Goer and would go-the-whole-way on the next date. I went All the Way to the bus stop with him and waved him off. Hah!

I would like to say I had no regrets about this

but I was V. Worried about it. I hadn't enjoyed kissing Simon so was I a Lesbian? Or a Horsophile? And since I enjoyed kissing Benjy and Rover more, was I a paedophile? Or a Pussophile?

> **TIP:** How to Kiss. First, find a comfortable location, and one where you are not likely to be disturbed. Sitting on the edge of a 200 foot drop, or standing in the middle of the road are undesirable, due to growing interest in The Business reducing interest in general

Each night and every night, all over the world, Teenage Worriers are practising kissing (on their hands . . .)

survival. Open your mouth slightly (practise on your hand, kissing a closed mouth is like kissing a stone) and start with a little gentle lip-brushing without raising the stakes by raising the pressure. Then press a little harder, attempting to keep your nose out of the way of your partner's (difficult in the case of Moi) followed by the merest hint of tongue-to-tongue fondling, then (THE PUBLISHER REGRETS THAT DUE TO THE EXPLICIT NATURE OF THIS PASSAGE IT HAS BEEN DELETED AS UNSUITABLE FOR MINORS).

LATENESS

Ever noticed how the more Worried you are, the less punctual you are?

An unworried person shimmers smoothly from bed to bathroom to breakfast to bus as if walking on water.

A Worried person's start to the day: attempt to hurl alarm clock out of window at first peep (Worry about not getting enough Beauty sleep); wake ten minutes later in panic; leap out of bed, stepping on Clockwork Thing abandoned by small sibling; go back to bed, clutching foot and demanding X-rays, Etck; get up, due to Indifference of World; stumble to bathroom; worry about Furry tongue, greasy wig, cold sores, Etck; wonder if mirror is actually reflecting Self, or if looking out of window at murder victim; start fresh Worries about WHAT TO WEAR;

try everything in wardrobe; take it all off again except what is too tight to be removed in less than three hours training at Houdini Escapology School; dump everything on floor; hurtle towards breakfast. Too late.

Fly. Three times our heroine hurtles from the house. Three times she returns. Once to check murder victim in bathroom isn't still there; once because she realizes she is wearing a Rupert Bear T-shirt; once because she has forgotten her Maths book. She races to the bus stop, slowed down by effort to avoid cracks in pavement, and is not surprised to see three number Nines cuddling each other at the stop. Will one wait for her? She fumbles nervously for her lucky rabbit's foot, but it is not in any of her pockets. It is not in her bag either. Tragedy!

> **TIP:** Don't go back for your lucky rabbit's foot.
> Try to remember you are a rational human being with
> A Will. Try to get out of habit of leaving for any
> destination at the time you are supposed to be arriving
> there. Remember Perversity of Malevolent Universe
> which throws obstacles in the way of any Late Person
> to make things worse.

NB. It is OK to be a little bit late in the Early Stages of A Relationship. Some strange people (not Moi though) are put off by partners who look too keen. NB Also: animal lovers please note that my rabbit's foot isn't real. The gypsy told me it would still work though.

**Assorted Teenage Worriers realizing they are wearing
Rupert Bear T-shirts**

Until Fred Kool makes it look GOOD GOOD GOOD

LEGS

Using just two legs instead of four like Rover (and, until recently, Benjy) has put us ahead of the game in the Animal Kingdom, since the arms are thus free for Hunting and Gathering, Passionate Gropings, DIY, Etck. But although legs are for letting the rest of your body develop a free and independent lifestyle, you wouldn't know it when it comes to being a Girl in a Man's World. Firstly, girls are endlessly shaving them (see ARMPITS), secondly, though they get banged about just as much in the general hurly-burly, your knees are supposed to look like marble polished by a thousand artisans, and then you're supposed to cover them in slinky stuff which always rips the first time you put it on.

If you do not succumb to this and wear trousers and socks like boys you will get by most of the time. But come weddings, poshish parties, etck someone (usually your mother) is bound to say sooner or later 'Why don't you EVER WEAR A DRESS?' If you think this doesn't apply to you

Boo

163

and that we can do as we like these days, show me famous women on State Occasions, in Parliament, opening hospitals, Etck wearing trousers. I have legs like a boy anyway. I wonder if maybe I am turning into a hermaphrodite, what with that and the two hairs on my chest and the absence of buzooms.

LESBIAN

As far as I can see from the nice lesbian couple my parents know and the way they talk about their friends, lesbianism is often just the sort of trusting, soulful, homely relationship that a lot of het. partnerships aren't. Lesbianism is also a good bet for avoiding AIDS and much as I swoon for my Beloved with Hair the Colour of Wet Sand it's hard to deny that the average Girls are put together better than the average Boyz with all their bristles, bulgy muscles, hair on their backs, strange protuberances, Etck. However I do not really fancy Girls, so that's that. And of course some teachers are still too scared by loony religious people to talk about being gay in case they are fired, blacklisted, tortured Etck. This is V. Cruel to Teachers but more cruel to yoof, who are forced to ring helplines if they are Lesbian or Gay. See also GAY.

With Parents like this who needs enemies?

LIPS

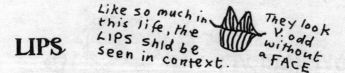

Like so much in this life, the LIPS shld be seen in context.

They look V. odd without a FACE

V. Important facial accessories. The eyes may be windows to the soul but of course Lips are windows to the intestines, which is not V. Romantic.

165

However, they are also used for smiling, grimacing, Etck (Body Language) and for the expression of Passionate Interest (See KISSING). My Lips are V. Thin and long. They do not resemble Cupid's bow so much as two of his arrows stuck together and a bit bent at the ends. They also get lots of black bits stuck on them (does this happen to anyone else? I've never noticed it. Does everyone else pick their black bits off? Or is this part of being a hermaphrodite? Maybe I'm from another planet. If only it was Krypton, but it's obviously the planet Blurge, a horrible slurpy place full of zit-contents, scabs, green goo, Etck. If Superman came from here he'd look like a colossal Bogey in a cape, which would have made quite a difference to his movies at the box office, I shd think).

TIP: Try and forget about your lips, except when Kissing, and even then they tend to take care of things themselves. Girls shouldn't pout, it makes them look V. Dated, like pin-ups from WWII, though a Madonna look, which tells boys to Come and Get it and Get Lost at the same time, is worth working on.

LOVE (LURVE)

Aaaaaaaaaaaaaaah. Or Arrrrrrrrrrrrrgh. Depending on your mood. Most days I alternate between

Aaaaaaaaaaaaaaah and Arrrrrrrrrrrrrrrrgh (so fast over Daniel's lost letter I sometimes couldn't tell my aah's from my elbow, ha!).

I am finding the combination of Lurve and school V. Difficult. I do not get much work done. I cannot do Eng Lit without getting soppy over the romantic bits. Geography makes me think of blue seas and far-off isles on which I entwine with DH. French is V. Diff as it puts me in mind of French kisses, Letters, Etck and also the words 'Je t'aime'

The Effect of Lurve on the Essay

Lurve: its effect on Teenage Worriers

give me strong Urges. Biology is most
disconcerting of all.

Other aspects of life are tricky just
now too.

Love is V. Exhausting. Sometimes I
would rather not be in it. Before you know it
you've Fallen Right In and you can't get out. You
look at other couples squirming about on park
benches and feel even weepier, because your
Beloved is at a poncey boarding school and you are
Driven Apart.

Lurve: its effect on the Flower

I have written down everything Daniel said to me and it is all really brilliant. He has such insight, depth and warmth. Also I am V. Attached to the tilt of his nose, the slant of his shoulder and the little lock of hair that he keeps brushing off his eyes. I could probably count the hairs in this lock, just from memory. I pore over his handwriting (paw over it also, swoon, wriggle, Etck), it is so full of intellect and imagination.

If you are throwing up by now, I sympathize.

TIP: If worried about falling in love, do not worry, you will know when it happens. It is not like that feeling you get when you kiss a pop-star poster when

169

you are twelve. Nor is it like rubbing your face in Dobbin's mane as I have now discovered. It is more like sunrises, volcanoes and other extremities of the Planet on which, if only we all loved each other (swoon), we could dance, sing, kiss and sip strawberry milkshake all day long amid the palm trees and rustling waterfalls or ride wild horses at full gallop through leafy glades, Etck.

NB. I have Revised my opinions of Lurve since finishing this book. You will see why when you get to the end. But in the interests of honesty the publishers have persuaded me to leave this moving account of First Lurve (huh!) intact.

LUCK

'Born under a Bad Sign, been down since
I could crawl. If it wasn't for Bad Luck,
I wouldn't have no Luck at all.'

This is a famous Blues, by Blind Willy Lemon or somebody like that. I don't think V. Worried people are usually Lucky, because you have to seize on opportunities and Worriers can't react fast enough to seize on anything except rabbits-foot charms, today's star-charts, sedatives, Etck. V. Open, happy people are often Lucky, but maybe it's the other way round. V. Beautiful people are often lucky too, because they tend to get offered nice jobs, sports cars, holidays in Bermuda, wild nights of Passion, Etck. However, I tell myself that at least I have a roof over my head and three meals a day (more or less). This induces a mega outbreak of Poverty-Worry and Guilt at all the little children born to suffer.

This guilt, if harnessed like electricity, could probably power the world. Unharnessed it just keeps psychiatrists in work. Luckily the guilt seems to wear off as you get older, so although everybody is just as poor and starving, you don't Worry so much about it All Being Your Fault. Still it is harder to be Lucky if you are poor and starving, so maybe it's best to consider yourself V. Lucky if you are not these things since so many people in the world are, and treat anything else as a Bonus. See also THIRD WORLD DEBT.

CHAPTER EIGHT (MN)

*My parents are not speaking. The encyclopaedias
and the dishwasher have gone back. I pointed
out we were lucky to have a dishwasher
at all, never mind encyclopaedias, and as
Benjy noticed, the encyclopaedia doesn't have
Superman in it. My father said the working
classes needed Education and Luxury just like
everyone else. My mother said WORKING
classes in a very nasty way. She is out late all
the time.*

*I have persuaded her to put a blanket down on
the kitchen floor to stop Benjy having nightmares.
It is v. hard to hoover.*

*I sent Daniel my photos. He thinks they are
brilliant. I am seeing him on Saturday! Half term!
My cup runneth over!*

FRIDAY:
*I can't believe it! Both my parents are going out on
Saturday! How unbelievably selfish! They say I
HAVE to find a babysitter for Benjy if I am going
out and will NOT let Daniel come here while they
are out!*

*Thank God for Aggy, she is going to babysit.
She is a Saint and with all her troubles too (guilt,*

guilt). I will try to distract myself from the Promise of Paradise by getting on with the Ms.

MACHISMO

Many Boyz expect that they will be thought of as Wimps if they don't do a number of V. Strange things including: shouting V. Loudly to communicate with someone six inches (15 cm) away; puffing out their chests; clenching biceps, teeth and fists and eyelids; swaggering (hips, shoulders, eyebrows); talking in Grunts, Slobbers, Etck. Communication with these Gorillas can be more trying than with a real Gorilla.

Well, if you want to look like one, it's a free country in that respect anyway, but the most Sexy, Interesting and Intelligent Girls (ie Moi) don't go for it much. Sexy Girls who are not Interesting or

Sadly Lurve is sometimes Blind

Intelligent sometimes do, and that is often quite enough for Macho Boyz who have trouble speaking, thinking Etck anyway, and certainly can't cope with it from Mere Girls.

> **TIP:** If you fancy someone but you are worried he might be Macho, ask yourself if he has a sensitive side and all the other stuff is just a phase, because he's Insecure as a Man, esp with his Mates. But if he's just as Macho when you're alone together as he is down the pub and he thinks things you Like/Believe In, Etck aren't important, he probably doesn't really like Girls all that much. Better to take a cold shower and go to bed with a packet of Smarties.

MAGAZINES

Buy one and before you know it, three hours have gone. If you added the amount of time I have spent reading identical articles on make-up, dating, music, horoscopes, etck etck, I could have helped even MORE old ladies over the road than in the time I spend looking in a mirror. This is v. worrying, but we must have our pleasures, and what would this mortal coil be if all we had was duty. Where would I be without *Smirk* Etck.

I suspect that I would have a lot more MONEY.

I would also have a lot less old sachets of face cream, dandruff-removing shampoo and kohl

Anticipation

Frustration

One week later: Renewed Hope

eyeliners that come FREE taped on the front of *Tru-Luv*, Etck. But addiction runs in families. With my father it's Newspapers. He nags me about the krap I read. But look at the krap he reads, and all written by young Oxbridge fogeys in sports jackets too! Plus some 4 million grown-ups read the *Sun*, which suggests that the Human Race may not be worth saving by the likes of idealistic types such as Daniel and Moi.

Still, I have it in mind to try to resist the following blandishments in the New Year:

'16 SENSATIONAL MAKE-UP TIPS', 'TREAT YOURSELF TO TONS OF FASHION!', 'MAKE ALL YOUR WILDEST DREAMS COME TRUE!'

Because although these headlines have come on every single copy of *Smirk*, my wildest dreams have not come true and I dare *Smirk* to give us the phone numbers of the people who can prove this statement. I bet they can't (seethe, hiss, boo).

MEANING OF LIFE

Major Worry of all Thinking Teenagers. The most surprising thing is how few thinking adults seem to worry about the Meaning of Life at all. The main worries are the Big Four Questions:

1) Where Did We Come From?
2) Where Are We Going To?

3) Why Are We here?

4) What's It All About, Anyway?

But just try asking an adult any of this stuff. If
Benjy asks these Big Qs he gets V. Dinky answers
accompanied by admiring looks and suggestions
that he may be a Genius. If I ask them, it only
reveals how long ago most adults' brains turned
to cold porridge and they stepped on to the
treadmills they have pedalled away at ever since,
just like Horace. When you're older, you're
NOT SUPPOSED TO ASK ANY MORE.
Because NOBODY KNOWS. Naturally there
are Clever-Clogs responses to all of these, eg:

1) Your parents had sex and you were born.

2) To the graveyard, ducky.

3) See Number One above.

4) Trying to Stay Alive.

It is v. sad to be a teenager and to cast off the
radiant trusting dream of infancy and realize there
are no easy answers. It is even more sad to see
how little time adults have to contemplate the rich
variety of this wondrous planet, and the Noble
Universe in all its Glory, Etck.

But although I Worry a lot about the Meaning
of Life I can already feel it fading (not life, the
worrying). Because I no longer lie on my back on
the grass trying hard to fall into the sky and understand Infinity. I do not think this is because I am
getting old, it is more to do with Hay Fever.

But if there is an Infinite number of everything
then there must be an infinite number of planets

Meaning of Life

EXACTLY LIKE OURS. And an infinite number of planets a Teeny bit different from ours. And an infinite number of Letty Chubbs exactly like me. And an infinite number of Letty Chubbs a teeny bit different. And an infinite number of Daniel Hopes (swoooooooooon). And an infinite number of Daniel Hopes and Letty Chubbs Falling In Lurve, or Splitting Up, or Not Even ever Meeting Each Other (TREMBLE). And I don't know whether I am one of the Lucky Letty Chubbs or the UNlucky Letty Chubbs in this picture. And whether I have any say in the matter anyway.

When you start to think like this, your brain hurts, so it is not surprising most people stop it fairly young while their brains are still quite springy.

The main problem with the Meaning of Life (apart from it keeping me awake at nights) is that Politicians, Religious Leaders, etck often confuse it with the search for Happiness which they also don't like to do anything about. But the Meaning of Life, as Teenage Worriers know, is to do with tip-toeing up to the ABYSS. And LOOKING IN. And as someone once said: Shine a torch into darkness and it just shows you how much more darkness there is still to be looked at. Yeech.

TIP: Aggy has told me that I must read *A Brief History of Time* to understand some of this better. I am v. scared of Time, but I will try. Maybe I will read it and *The Koran* next year instead of *Smirk*.

MENSTRUATION

I used to think it V. Sexist that this wasn't called Womenstruation, but have since discovered it comes from the Latin word 'Mensis', meaning month. V. Humbling. If I had gone to a posh school I would probably have known this a long time ago.

You rent your garments at the loss
of Childish Innocence

It is also called the Curse (by my gran), Periods,
Monthlies, Etck Etck. In fact it is a quite exciting
thing as it is the bod's way of shedding all the little
eggs from the inside of the womb, where, if they
were fertilized, they would stay and turn into
babies. Hazel started her periods V. Early, at 11.
Aggy was 13 and I was 14½. This meant I was
V.V.V. Worried about not being a woman until
last year. I am still a bit worried I might be a
hermaphrodite. I wore a press-on pad from the age
of 11, just in case I came on, but in retrospect I
wouldn't recommend the expense over a four-year

period (ho ho), although they are much easier to use at first than tampons and you don't lie awake Worrying that you might have forgotten to take last month's one out.

Once you actually get your periods, of course, the excitement wears off V. Quickly and you rent your garments at the loss of Childish Innocence, etck grrr so you can't win. (Also, I couldn't find anyone who wanted to rent my garments, or even pay a small deposit on them, hah!)

It is a shame that in the 21st century periods are STILL embarrassing. It is V. Imp to campaign for tampon and towel machines in all the public loos and also to offer tampons freely to your

Do you Tampon?

Men do not suffer from P.M.T.

friends (less damaging than fags and twice as funny).

NB. If your school bag fell on the floor and 4,000 tampons fell out why would you be more embarrassed than if 4,000 tissues fell out?

If your answer was you wouldn't be embarrassed, I award you the Letty Chubb Excellent Achievement Scroll for 21st Century Womanhood or V. Good Liar – tick where applicable.

Men used to use women's periods as an excuse for not giving them Top Jobs, on the grounds that they would be V. Ratty and unpredictable Once A Month. Men, including my father, are often V. Ratty and Unpredictable as a result of hangovers, wounds to their Egos, strange noises from the car, Etck about 20 times a month, so So What?

Personally, I do not suffer from PMT (Pre-Menstrual Tension) at ALL. I just get V.V.V. Ratty a couple of days before my period is due.

My mother always says: 'You are V. Ratty, your period must be due,' and I flounce off claiming that she has no understanding of the agonies of my SOUL. Later, I sometimes conclude she was right, but I don't tell her.

It is a shame you can't use periods as an excuse to get off games, swimming, etck any more unless you have V. Bad cramps, which I don't.

MONEY

I have been trying to make money since I was 9. The first money I made was a five pound note done with a V. Fine pen and blue ink. The sweet-shop lady kindly gave me a packet of Polos but NO CHANGE. She said the ingenuity was worth the Polos and she would frame it. I bet she didn't work three weeks for the price of a packet of Polos. When I'm famous that L. Chubb fiver will be worth at least £6.

When I was 10 I made horses out of modelling clay and flogged them to my friends. But their legs kept snapping off (the horses, yeah, not my friends) and after making eight of them I wound up with

The first money I made was when I was nine

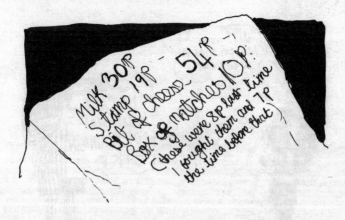

Granny Chubb's Account From 10 Years Ago

10p profit. Granny Chubb still has her two in a glass cabinet. They are the only things she doesn't dust.

At 14 I did a Sunday paper round for three weeks. OK, I couldn't carry them. YOU try it.

So now I make do with the pittance my parents give me. It keeps me in copies of *Smirk* etck and that's my lot. They don't give me much because they say they are so Worried about Money. The only relief they get from it is boozing and smoking and going out.

Granny Chubb notes down everything she spends on corners of paper torn from used envelopes, with little notes attached viz: 'Milk 60p, stamp 21p, one sausage 50p, box of matches 45p (these were 40p last time I bought them and 37p the time before that. Must write to Dept of Unfair Trading) Etck. But if she went to a

185

The Enterprise Culture . . .

bank for an overdraft (she'd rather hang herself)
they'd refuse. If people in suits with shiny
brochures and calculators, Etck go, they get
showered with millions of pounds, which they
spend on furry carpets, pink telephones, girls in
high heels, Etck, come back for more to run the
business with, become bankrupt, change their
names, and start again. This is called Confidence.

MUSIC

Daniel is musical. A funny look comes over him when he listens to music he likes. I think the same look comes over his face when we are entwined (Swooon), but I'm too close up to be able to tell for certain. He also understands about Music, which I don't.

I do believe, however, that Music has healing powers, brings people together, etck. I could see

Rover having her bi-annual Worry

this watching Dad's old home movie of all the
people standing in binliners, in the rain, watching
Pavarotti in the Park next to the PM, Princess Di,
Etck. Most people had the same look as Daniel
gets on his face and I found it V. Moving. He got
the words wrong to *Just One Cornetto* of course,
but to true Music lovers, if it is not about Icecream
it is but a Mere Trifle (hah!).

My parents think the new dance music sounds
like old typewriters. They also disapprove of
Classical Music being marketed like scent, clothes,
Etck, with pix of V. Beautiful people playing cellos,
waving batons and NOT dressed up as penguins.
However, I do not mind because it seems to me
that music is becoming more democratic, not just
Classical and Opera for people called Petronella
and Tarquin and pop for people called Sharon
and Tel.

Daniel says really interesting Music for the
last 50 years has been ripped off from Working
People, the Third World, Etck – rock 'n' roll was
invented by Black Americans but marketed by
boyz looking like James Dean (phew, clash of
loyalties). 'World Music' is all nicked from
Africa, Latin America and the East and then
recycled on synthesizers. Apparently Mozart,
Etck were all early pop stars who would have
hated the idea of their music being played to
audiences who sat around looking like shop-
window dummies.

TIP: Music-Worry is usually caused by either hating it when everyone else seems to love it or vice versa. If you are scared of people laughing at you, you can either keep stum about not having enjoyed any music since 'Humpty Dumpty' or find someone to share your tastes. This is even true if you like Heavy Metal.

NAILS

I have been biting mine since I can remember. My mother says it's because she didn't breast-feed me for long enough (guilt, whinge, lash). Maybe analysis in future years will prove her right. But I think this theory is a sexist plot designed to chain women to the cradle, although only breast-feeding me for two days was a bit stingy when she did Benjy for SIX MONTHS.

Menu
Cuticle curry
Talon on Toast
Claws in aspic
Nails & Chips
Cold Clippings
Fried Filings

Nail-Biting Worrier

I do not want talons like Cruella de Vil but I wouldn't mind nice oval-type pearly ones as worn in *Tru-Luv* photo sessions.

NAMES

As a victim of *Gone With the Wind* I sympathize with all those with Name-Worries. I'm amazed how names are never taken into consideration in explaining why someone commits crimes or goes mad. Parents who name their children after heroes and heroines or Greek literature (resulting in tragedies like seven-stone spindly weeds called Apollo) should be given terrible Punishment like being forced to appear on Game Shows. Granny Gosling says she nearly named one of my mother's brothers Crocus because there was one in a pot by her bed after the birth. This is the kind of thing we are up against, before we have a say in anything. People with dodgy surnames usually do a bit of tinkering, ie if you are called Botham or Bottome it is likely your ancestors were Bottoms.

TIP: Whether you are a gross victim of Naming-Terror, like Gloria Sidebottom, or a more subtle one, like Tamara Knight, learn to love your name (wish I could). Or as Groucho Marx once said: 'You're a disgrace to our family name of Wagstaff – if such a thing is possible.'

NECKS

V. Imp for twining round neck of beloved (ie necking). I feel sorry for stumpy people with no necks, but mine is so bendy that it is V. Hard work keeping my head up, like the flamingo croquet mallets in *Alice in Wonderland*. I used to measure it as I was scared I was turning into one. But it has definitely not grown any longer in the last eight days, so I won't measure it again for a week.

Was I turning into a Flamingo?

NERVES

These are little bundles of fibres through which your brain talks to the rest of you. Older people talk about them a lot, as in 'Her nerves are very bad.' I hate to think what mine will be like if I live to draw a pension (if there are any pencils left to draw it with by then. Hah!). My mother said I was a jumpy baby. That's the kind that looks like a demented starfish at the sound of a cat washing. I still hate the sound of the hoover and leap into the air whenever the phone rings. If Benjy puts on a scary mask I scream. I had to be taken out of *The Postman Pat Show for Tiny Tots* when I was SIX.

It would be V. Good not to have nerves and therefore not to be nervous. On the other hand, without them you would not be able to tell if you were on fire or had lost a leg. According to old Brit War-movies, many of the officers as played by John Mills, Etck are not able to tell these things (Having Nerves-of-Steel) and thus are Good Chaps in Tight Corners.

> **TIP:** People of a V. Nervous disposition like myself and Benjy (aaaaah! Bless!) can comfort themselves by knowing that they are V. Brave indeed, even to get up in the morning.

NIPPLES

All humans and many animals have nipples but the nipples of the female human have assumed a Worry Quotient quite out of proportion to their size, importance and place in the Universe. Their purpose, of course, is to give the human infant its first experience of Fast Food, but papers like the *Sun* find this a V. Inconvenient fact and try to forget about it. Instead, they try to make us Worry what our nipples LOOK like. Once you start thinking about this (Boyz do, a lot) you find nipples come in all shapes, colours and sizes. Pointing Up, Down, In and Sideways. Some are v. big, some are titchy. All are normal. Hooray. But is it a comfort being Normal? (see below)

Anyway, soon you will probably be able to buy realistic ones to pop on over your real ones. Will it change your life? If the answer is yes, you need some Outside Interests like working for the poor and needy. (Maybe I could be an Agony Aunt if film directing doesn't work out . . .)

Think of ME, for instance. I don't even have any buzooms!!!! Count yourself lucky you've got something to put your nipples ON!!!!

NORMAL

As in, *'Don't worry, it's perfectly normal at your age.'* 'Perfectly normal' is the phase Doctors, Teachers, Agony Aunts, Etck thrive on.

It is Perfectly Normal to have spots, nightmares, stomachaches, titchy Willies, six chins, divorced parents, broken hearts, Etck Etck.

But just because other people might be in the same boat it hardly makes it less of a WORRY. If I've got Spots I'm not Worried about whether it's Normal or not, I'm Worried about whether there's a tube of something that will fix it, same as Yoof with Divorced Parents want a tube of something to stick them together again.

I don't want to be Perfectly Normal and I don't want to know anyone who does. I am a profoundly Important, Subtle, Complex, Brilliant, Tortured, Misunderstood INDIVIDUAL. No one has ever felt like me in the history of the WORLD, written so many poems or been SO anguished about Spots, Lurve, Etck.

I would like to sponsor a Radio Soap Opera that goes like this:

THE BLANDS – AN EVERYDAY STORY OF ABNORMAL FOLK (Signature tune dum-di-dum).

Normal Teenagers . . .

. . . having a Little Worry

The Bland family live in a spacious, yet cosy house w. four delightful teenage children, rabbits and a faithful hound. The children all work V. Hard at school, are V. Polite and love writing Thank-You letters. They also love sitting reading by the log fire, cooking supper for their tired but successful Dad, and accompanying their parents to Church on Sunday, followed by a picnic by a dappled brook. The boys play gentle cricket. Thwap. Clunk. Dramas unfold! A thorn is extracted from an incy furry creature's paw, a ball is retrieved from the babbling brook. The family motor home to roast beef and crunchy Yorkshire pud and enjoy a quiet game of Cluedo round the piano.

It is a thing V. Sad that eventually the Bland Family all die of Lassa fever and their pets starve in a slow agony of neglect, but it is no more abnormal than anything else in the show.

NOSE *(A nose by any other name could smell your feet. Hah!)*

Important bit in the middle of your face. Essential for checking pongs eg sweat and halitosis. Mine is V. Pointy. Aggy's is blobby. Hazel's is V. Short and straight with sculpted nostrils. Ditto Daniel's (swoooooooon). Granny Chubb's is blunt with a wart

When attempting to redesign the NOSE, I envisaged a small
internal TAP manned (I mean personned) by ELVES (or do I
mean Elved?) HOWEVER . . . where would all the SNOT go
to, if it didn't DRIP? Even if the Elves had BUCKETS, where
would they EMPTY them? Worry, worry.

on. Benjy's nose pickings are ranged all down the
side of his bed along with bits of chewing gum.

The nose is a big LOOKS worry. I have dreamed
of plastic surgery which kind parents in the USA give
their daughters as BIRTHDAY PRESENTS, but I
couldn't stand the mockery from my Alleged Friendz,
nor going round with two black eyes for weeks. I no
longer need a nose for tracking food, scenting danger,
Etck, so why has Evolution played this cruel trick? If
I could get hold of that Charles Darwin I'd give him
a piece of my nose, and no mistake.

**TIP: Pointy and bumpy proboscis sufferers
should simply avoid turning profiles to those they
love and to cameras.**

I have perfected a V. Unobtrusive head-swivelling technique which renders my proboscis a blur

NUCLEAR

Usually applied to V. Horrible Bombs capable of reducing planet to fine dust, Etck. Enough of them built to blow up entire Solar System when Capitalists feared Communists and vice versa but now almost everyone is trying to be Capitalist they aren't wanted any more, except by little countries run by loony soldiers who want to scare their neighbours. I Worry that the universal attempt to be Capitalist will make lots of people even Poorer and Crosser and even less likely to care about blowing us all up. As for Nuclear Reactors (viz: eco-friendly Chernobyl, Etck) and Safe Clean Energy (pah, pull-the-other-one), give me Wind, Waves and Sun any day. (Plus nice beach, Daniel, Milk Shake Etck.)

This is the point where you have to rope in the Teenage Think Tank (and probably the Toddler

Biggest Worry in World Dept.

Think Tank too) and work out a safe future. It is a V. Good exercise but induces mega-readings on the Worryometer because it is still a V. Big Problem. In fact the biggest in the world.

NUMBERS

I don't like having odd shirt buttons or even being 15. (14 was better and 13 – aaaaargh – made me hysterical.) I see numbers in colour and all the odd ones are sort of greeny-greyish and all the even ones are rosey-goldish. I expect it's to do with some sort of maths chart I had above my cot. That's pushy parents for you.

CHAPTER NINE (OP)

*The big night! Cinema! Meal! Daniel and I are
as one with each other. He said he would like
to see more of me in a V. Exciting voice. If I
am not allowed to see him EVERY DAY in the
Christmas Holidays I will ELOPE. (I hope he
comes too.)*

*Arrived back late to find my parents not home
yet! Their selfishness is unbelievable. Aggy in tears
because her father will be mad at her for being so
late. She had no money for a cab and fled weeping
into the night.*

*Poor Aggy. I feel so bad for her. I am V. Worried
about my parents. They got back SEPARATELY
at 2am and 3am. It was a Supreme Effort not to
go down and ask what they thought they meant
by arriving home at this hour. Are they seeing
someone else?*

*Benjy dreamt the blanket was a bearskin rug
which came alive and ate Horace. I had him in
my bed to comfort him in the absence of his only
parents. Does he need to see a Shrink or is it just
his age?*

OLD PEOPLE

I am V. Worried about Old People in today's hurly burly with the economy going down the plug hole and pension funds stolen by bandits in Armani suits, Etck. (Even the investigators of frauds get £300 an HOUR, per *Yuke*!)

I like to think I worry about the Aged because I am a warm and wonderful person but I think it has more to do with my v. great affection for Granny Chubb who does not have two pennies to rub together (but if she did she would spend them on Gleamo).

Join Letty Chubb's Crinklies' Campaign: Turbo-powered wheelchairs on demand! Free Bimbo! (*Shouldn't this be Bingo? – Ed*). Free transport all over the world on Jumbo Jets in special OAP-class compartments, complete with bedpans, WWII movies, Frank Sinatra records, Etck. Even Real Old Horrors shall be cuddled and given posh kit, just like little Toddler Horrors always are.

I wonder whether I should get the Teenage Think Tank to prioritize this over The Nuclear Bomb? It is V. Worrying, but if I add up the time I spend listening to Granny Chubb it is probably only about half a day a year. SHE listens to ME much more (guilt). Lash.

See also GRANDPARENTS.

OXYGEN

Essential item for maintenance of life on planet Earth. Major Worry is, will it RUN OUT? In London it has nearly gone already and people are advised to stay in if there isn't a stiff breeze. There are probably other planets where Life meanders on V. Pleasantly without it and everyone has gills like fish, or breathes noxious gases quite happily. Perhaps we will mutate. Benjy, for instance, has always been able to breathe noxious gases quite happily, most of them made by him.

NB. I wonder if the air we breathe has been around since history began? If so, since you've been reading this you've probably gulped a few mouthfuls that were breathed in and out by Hitler, Stalin and Attila the Hun already. Maybe this is why previously Good people suddenly Turn Bad. If you could filter it, and market it as Air Breathed By Saints Only, you could make a fortune (I mean, improve the lot of humankind).

OZONE

Even more worrying than oxygen just now, because Ozone is stuff that acts like a sun-cream up in the sky and stops us being scorched to a cinder. It is

getting V. Thin and Holey. This is because we use aerosols, drive cars and have fridges, Etck. It is V.V. Selfish but with public transport so bad, underarm sweat so bad and salmonella danger so bad it is difficult to sacrifice short-term gain for the Good Of the Community at Large (lash, guilt, hair socks, Etck).

A Good Govt inspired by the Teenage Think Tank would make a few more laws about such things and everyone would moan and buckle down. I for one would be quite happy to eat fresh food bought and prepared daily by my mother if only she would do it.

See also ENVIRONMENT.

PACIFISM

Worrying because although it is V. Easy to be a pacifist like me it is not so easy when you think

Hitler might have ruled if our forefathers and mothers had stood by, picking their hooters. Also, I am not always a Pacifist. When Alison Shrivel pulled my hair I hit her with a rolled-up copy of *Smirk*, though unfortunately I forgot there was an Aerosol of Fugplug underarm deodorant wrapped up in it. The only reason Bullies do not rule the playground is because the Fearless Few resist them and I have a feeling the same goes for the Rest of the World. Tragickally, as recent events have proved, you might think that you are going for a Bully and end up as a Bully Yrself.

Of course, if you ask either a child of 6 or a 19-year-old whether it's a good idea to pour burning oil on Babies you can bet the answer from both is going to be No. Yet that is what lots of 19-year-old men did in the Vietnam war and they have done similar stuff in every war ever since. This is one of those V. Big conundrums, ie the diff between the individual who is Quite Pleasant, Kind and takes boy scouts out of horses' hooves, Etck and the same individual when in a Mob, which armies often become if they think nobody's watching.

NB. My mother is fond of urging Benjy to take his 'latent aggression' out on a beanbag. So the Arms Manufacturers could also deploy their workforce in making Vast ones to put along the borders of the World's Nations.

PAINTING

I am V. Worried about my Mother's obsessive desire to paint instead of look after us. I am a Feminist but there are limits when you come home to a cold house with your father curled up in a heap of newspapers and the kitchen ceiling has fallen down and your poor baby brother (aaaaah bless!) is crying for his toast and Marmite.

It's time for more women to have a goat (*shouldn't there be a word space here – Ed.*) splashing the old oils about. But does my Darling Mother paint Adonises covered in primroses? No, she does big blobby things that look like bogeys on a microscope.

PALMISTRY

Aggy and I had our palms read this summer. The woman was a direct descendant of Gypsy Rose Lee and the man who came out in front of us said she was brilliant. She was, too. She told me there were two men in my life, one dark, one fair (Brian and

Daniel, swooooon) and that one would turn out to be V. Imp to me (how V. True). That I would cross water soon (I had to walk back along the pier, so she was right about that, too) and that, although she hoped I didn't mind her saying so (I got V. Nervous at this point), she was going to give me some V. Serious Advice (by now I was rigid with terror). She reckoned that I had been too hard on myself and should take it easy and stop helping other people so much and look after myself a bit more. How V.V. True and kind and perceptive of her that was.

My spirits were somewhat dampened by Aggy who had been told EXACTLY the same things. And there were no men in Aggy's life at all. She had also been told to go easy on herself.

I am V. Worried about my lifeline, even so. Also my fate-line which is non-existent and means I will have no career . . . Also, I know this is a V. Creepy thought and I'm too superstitious almost to say it, but I wonder if any palmists have ever looked at the palms of, um, well, people who are no longer BREATHING, to see if their lifelines indicate the time of their demise.

PANDAS

V. Worrying. Tragic beast, because V. Cuddly but
not keen enough on Doing It to survive, it seems. A
diet of Bamboo probably doesn't help. Taking it on
a lead to the nearest McDonald's sounds a much
better idea.

PARENTS

Constant source of Worry to the average teenager,
who either does not have enough of them (ie single-
parent families, orphans, Etck), or too many
(ie second and third marriages, wicked stepfathers,
Etck). Wicked Stepfathers are in fact more common
than Wicked Stepmothers despite the propaganda
put around by V. Sexist fairy tales (and also my
father's dictionary, published 1976, which lists
Stepmothers as 'harsh or neglectful', but not
Stepfathers). Stepfathers are often far from interested
in their stepchildren and want to Grope all over their
Hallowed Mother instead which is V. Disgusting to a
self-respecting son or daughter (see *Hamlet* for more
on this, which proves yet again the relevance of the
Bard to Yoof Today). They also sometimes make
passes at the sons and daughters on the grounds that
it's not incest if you're not related. No one should
have to put up with this for a millisecond.

Parents (sample 1)

Parents (sample 2)

Ring CHILDLINE straight away if anything like this happens to you from anyone AT ALL!!!! NB: In the interests of Honesty I should add that there are also a lot of V. Nice Stepparents of both sexes and a lot of V. Horrid 'Natural' Parents as most Teenage Worriers know only too well.

If you are adopted you now have a right to find your 'real' parents. This could be V. Interesting especially if you turned out to be a king or something but it is more likely that you would turn out to be even more of a pauper than you are and also that your real real parents are the ones wot cared for you tenderly all these years.

But even in your average abnormal family of two married parents, they are a huge worry. They smoke and drink too much, they are out V. Late so you can't sleep for worrying. They have terrible rows and fits of deep depression. They sulk over breakfast with their heads buried in the newspaper. They are obsessed with Pension Plans, losing hair, jobs, waistlines, Urges Etck. They are ALWAYS in the bathroom when you need it, are reckless about safety and do not use back seat-belts in their cars. They care nothing for the environment and cannot be bothered to recycle bottles, newspapers, stamps or even make compost for their window boxes out of waste veg. When they are not hitting the bottle they are downing tea and coffee at an alarming rate.

They are selfish and have V. Little time for anyone but themselves. They are Irrational and Moody, play Horrible Music, have no idea whatever of the value of money, spend hours on the phone when you are expecting a V.V.V. Imp call, or else they don't pay the bill and the phone is cut off when you are expecting a V.V.V. Imp call. They are V.V. Demanding, always asking you to do things for them and to be nice to their friends and relatives. They are always tired.

Sometimes I wonder why we have them.

PARTIES

Endless source of Worry. What to wear; how to do the hair; whether to dance; how to dance; whether your True Love will be there alone, with someone, or not there at all; whether he or she will get off with someone under your Nose, or because of your Nose (See NOSE) Etck.

Secretly I am a bit scared of Parties. I am scared someone will slip me drugs in my cake or spike my cola. Ashley took something by mistake at a party once and thought he was a fountain pen. He spent 8 hours standing rigid behind a door terrified that someone would pick him up and write with him. I cannot drink because even the smell of alcohol makes me fall on my back and sing *Papa Don't Preach*. I'm certain it's caused by my undiagnosed glandular fever.

213

I have always secretly been a bit scared of parties – but I
don't let it show

I am also scared that some V. Lecherous smelly bloke will paw me, or that a V. Handsome witty and eloquent one won't.

I also look V. Silly when I am dressed up. I don't think I've found my STYLE, as they say in *Smirk*.

> **TIP:** If you have not found your STYLE, be V. Neutral. Mild eccentricities like a sprig of holly up the nostrils are only OK if you look like Hazel. You can get gold spray for hair which is v. good for both sexes and transforms your jeans and T-shirt into a party-type ensemble in seconds (maybe I could get a job on *Smirk*).
> If your True Lurve is with Another you have two options: pouring your drink over them or a dignified retreat. I would recommend both, except the retreat should be hasty.
> If you are stuffing peanuts while conversing, watch where you are getting them from. Brian once dipped his hand into a bowl and found himself with a mouthful of dogends. This is the sort of thing that would never happen to Daniel, but it might to you or me.

PATRIARCHY

This is a system in which the Father is the Ruler of the Family and the Man is Ruler of the World. Until recently this was the case everywhere, but

one-parent families, househusbands, women
Prime Ministers, Etck are changing the rules.
There used to be things called matriarchies when
women were on top, and I wouldn't mind them
coming back, but a better system would be where
everyone did bits of everything, like ruling, digging,
washing-up, changing nappies, playing football
(grrrr).

Lots of boys are still v. worried that their Willies
will drop off if they look after children or sew on a
button. This is v. odd because science has proved
the Willy to be firmly affixed.

POLITICS

Since most Yoof say they are not interested in
Politics (including Moi, until I started this book
and realized Politics affects virtually everything,
including how to clear up spots and how much
money, houses, etck you can expect to get), here is
Letty Chubb's MUGS GUIDE.

FASCISM starts by one group of people blaming
another group, usually foreigners, for everything
that's wrong. So they smash them up and then turn
on each other. Whoever wins becomes Dictator,
burns libraries, makes the trains run on time,
enlists almost everybody into the army and tortures
the remainder.

NB. *Shouldn't this be 'happiness'? – Ed.*

This might lead to COMMUNISM where the poor people rise up and smash things like rich people's cars and then read to them from V. Imp books they've managed to preserve under mattresses, until they understand how Bad it is to have more things than anyone else. When all the rich people's things have been distributed among the poor, nobody will need to work any more and the Govt will wither away. Factories building anything useful wither away too, because nobody has a good enough reason to make them work, so no one has anything, so someone has to be a Dictator all over again.

Or, you can have DEMOCRACY, which means One Person, One Vote. In this system you have: SOCIALISM (which is what the LABOUR PARTY used to be in favour of). Where Ordinary People still Rise Up, but only to read V. Imp Books to try and Persuade Rich people to hand over some dosh before they get their cars smashed, Etck. So everything will be fairer and we will all have an equal chance to be educated, cured, etck. Rich people do not like this so they prefer: CONSERVATISM (which is what the CONSERVA- TIVE PARTY used to stand for). Where rich people rise up and read to poor people from V. Imp newspapers like the *Sun* that they are safer being governed by People Who Know How, forgetting about boring things like Politics and concentrating on Page Three, Rooney, Etck. This upsets kind-hearted Middling people who opt for:

LIBERALISM, which is when Middling People sit around and chat to Rich people about how they should have a weeny bit less and to Poor People about how they might get a weeny bit more.

I think Winston Churchill may have been right when he said 'Democracy is the worst form of government – except for all the others.'

See also ENVIRONMENT, IDEAS, MEANING OF LIFE Etck, Etck.

PRAYING

Ever since I realized that both armies in a war do some praying to win (often to the same God) I have been V. Worried about its efficacy. The Communist Party in China used to tell children to close their eyes and pray V. Hard to God for icecream. Zilch. Then they said now pray V. Hard to the Communist Party for icecream. Surprise, surprise, just five billion Cornettos!

This is brain-washing, but are we brain-washed by all that incy Nativity Play stuff we get at Nursery School? Benjy's class did a great one last year. The Angel Gabriel had adenoids and asked Bary to lay the chide id a Banger.

See also GOD and RELIGION.

PREGNANCY

V. Worrying for anyone who has Done It, or
nearly Done It as Sperm (see SPERM) are persistent
little things and can find their way to an egg
faster than Benjy at breakfast time. For a long
time I thought the boy's Willy had to connect
with the girl's belly button which shows how sex
education can pass even a committed Worrier
by. But I wasn't so bad as Aggy's big sister,
who thought you could get pregnant by rubbing
noses.

I would recommend a condom plus cap, pill and
cream, but be sure to use at least one, anyway.
There's a test now to PROVE who the father is, so
watch out for maintenance payments, boys! You
too could be holding the baby. Waaaaaah.

There are also tests you can do v. early on (on
the day your period is due) and you can buy them
at the chemist. I have got a couple just in case.

NB. If you *do* get pregnant, get advice fast.
Preferably from an agency that doesn't think that
Teenagers who have abortions should boil in
Everlasting Oil.

See also BABIES, CONTRACEPTION,
MENSTRUATION, SEX, Etck.

CHAPTER TEN (QRS)

Long letter from Granny Gosling in V. Spidery handwriting. I had to borrow Benjy's magnifying glass to read it. It was all about putting my school-work first (moan moan) and not throwing myself away on the first man who comes along. (Like my mother did.) I can't believe my mother has told her about Daniel already. It is so insulting.

I have decided the only way to keep my family together is to make this Alphabet a best-seller. I am going to get Granny Gosling to give it to all her posh friends' grandchildren. She has at least enough money to buy ten copies which will give it a good start.

My father is V.V.V. Unhappy. He thinks my mother is Seeing Someone Else and it is forcing him to Drown His Sorrows. She says she isn't, but she bloody well will soon if he doesn't pull his finger out. (NB. Check origin of phrase, bet it's dirty.)

My bro, Ashley, rang to say he is getting married.

My mother is catatonic. My father says at least the girl's got money. My mother says that's what he thought about her. They row about everything at the moment, not least the bathroom. My father has taken the taps off for some piece he's writing for Classic DIY.

Tried rubbish bags on kitchen floor, but too noisy. Sent Daniel some of this book. I have removed his letters from under my pillow because they made me sneeze. His aftershave (YES! He SHAVES! Swoon) is a touch pervasive. Read some more of My Father's Great Work. The Man in the Shed's relationship with his dog has become very close. They Communicate in a language Unknown to Books. The dog teaches the Man to Track and Forage, and the Man teaches the dog to whittle sticks with its teeth. The Man begins to feel he is in touch with an Old Soul from which he can Learn Much. Thinks: Is this the Angry Young Man who trashed Lit Set complacency with Moving On?

QUEEN

It is V. sad to grow up and realize you are not going to marry a Prince and have a lot of Corgis. See ROYAL FAMILY and GAY.

RACISM

John Arlott, who apparently used to talk about Cricket on the radio, died and my Dad wore a

Ethnic Origins may well affect your chances of becoming a Cabinet Minister, Judge, Captain of Industry, Etck., Etck

Black armband for three months. When Arlott was asked to put his race down on a South African form he put 'HUMAN'. V. Good.

When I was in Juniors we had a teacher who told the whole class not to speak to any child with blue eyes for a whole day. The next day she did it with people with blond hair. We all got V. Upset but it was a V. Clever way of teaching us that the colours people are make no difference to what they are like.

One of my Father's friends came to England from the West Indies in the 60s when he was 12. He had read all of Charles Dickens and Shakespeare by then (!!!!) but when he got here all the white kids (who could hardly read a copy of the *Beano*) asked him why he didn't have a bone through his nose and wear a grass skirt?! He has never forgotten this.

It's a bit better now, according to Aggy, but nowhere near good enough. It is V.V.V. Scary and a V.V. Big Worry that some grown people can be so thick but hopefully the Teenage Think Tank will change all that even though some of the yobs in Year 11 remind me of Hitler. (And a few of them don't even know who Hitler was! Wise up ye Educators of Modern Yoof – at least if you want Us Lot to be better than Your lot.)

RADIOACTIVITY

V.V.V.V.V.V.V. Worrying because YOU CAN'T SEE IT. A lot of it fell all over the place when the Russian nuclear plant blew up, and there are always arguments about whether children living near nuclear plants get sick. I keep looking in my Father's *Exchange and Mart* for one of those little clicking things that measure the radioactivity, but I've never seen one advertised. Is this because the Govt is scared of us knowing the TRUTH?????

See also NUCLEAR.

RATS

There is a plague of Rats in the London sewers and one even came in our house last year and kept wandering into the living room to watch nature progs, Etck. The pest-control people use a kind of Animal-SAS undercover squad of V. Small blokes with whiskers. Do not get sentimental about Rats unless a Buddhist. My father eventually managed to hit ours with an iron bar, but he was V. Shocked by the experience and could not work for a week. If it wasn't for my allergies I would do more housework.

RECESSION

Someone once said that if all Economists were laid end to end they would not reach a conclusion, which is probably why adults argue about 'The Economy' and its failings with such, er, vehemence. Teenage Worriers like Moi would love to have it explained as we could lose our roofs from over our heads and be forced to beg. Lots of people are doing this already and they do not look like good candidates for the HAPPINESS SURVEY.

TIP: Make a lot of Money. Any ideas on this, please send me care of the Publisher. See also MONEY.

RELATIVES

These are the people you don't see all year until Christmas and then you realize why you haven't seen them all year. They like to bring you little incy Dollies even though you are FIFTEEN and sometimes they give you a pound, and act as if they've done something to change your life.

I think people have to pass exams in being relatives, where you learn to ask V. Silly questions and not wait for the answer, talk about people nobody else has heard of, get V.V.V. Interested in the directions from their house to yours, stay up late and eat all the mince pies.

Well Well Scarlett, you **HAVE** filled out nicely...

But they can be comforting because they have even pointier noses than you which makes you count your blessings. Also they would probably take you in if your entire family went down in an aeroplane. Not that this alleviates Flying Worries, but makes them much Worse.

RELIGION

There used to be just one big one in this country involving Jesus, but now there are lots so you can choose.

I am getting quite keen on Buddhism but the Greek Gods are quite appealing too (ie if one of

Religion: Infant School style. Starting as it means to go on?

Them doesn't like you, you can appeal to Another).

I have always held a V. Simple Belief, a bit like the 'Narnia' books, but the more I look at the Vale of Tears we inhabit the more I begin to Wonder. I think I may be turning into a Humanist which is a bit like being a Christian but without God. But I will miss God a bit if I do. It is upsetting.

Schools like Sluggs think they can get round this problem by ignoring Religion as much as poss. There is something to be said for this, since if you're not Religious you can't fight over it.

But since more people are killed in the names of various Gods than for any other reason I think the Educators of Yoof could do worse than try to explain why. If Jesus could see it all he'd turn in his cave.

See also GOD and PRAYING.

REPORTS

I get V.V.V. Worried about reports and tried to
forge one at about the same time I forged the five
pound note. I am always accused of talking too
much and not 'achieving my full potential'. Yet I
work my fingers to the bone for no pay.

My parents are too busy to care much anyway
although my mother collapses occasionally over
whether I 'fit in' and whether I shouldn't be
crammed with knowledge at a posh school at vast
expense. I don't think she even READ my last
report. Just as well.

ROMANCE

This is the bit before sex when you get
Valentines and flowers, Etck and Boyz pretend
to be interested in the Glorious Garden that is
your Soul (before attempting to whip the thin
winceyette from your pale and spotty bod). I have
sent a lot of Valentines but only ever got one
from Brian (yeeech) and my Aunt (double yeeeech).
That one was V. Disappointing as I thought it
was from Lionel who I had a big crush on when
I was 10.

Romance is something everyone does quite a lot
of thinking about but Boyz do not LET ON. In fact

**Graduates from the Letty Chubb School of
Positive Thinking**

a Boy I thought was dead boring and macho was
being V. Soppy on the bus the other day with a
Girl in Year 9. He didn't know I was behind but I
didn't laugh in case he hit me. Daniel is V.V.V.
Romantic I think. I can imagine the Valentines he is
bound to send me next year. Lots of them, all with
different handwriting. But I will KNOW.

See also LOVE.
(SWOOOOOOOOOOOOOOOOOOOOOOON.)

Sadly, he does not know she has hayfever

ROYAL FAMILY

Real-life Soap Opera only with bigger stars on
bigger incomes, that keeps Tourism flourishing
in ye Disneyland nation I belong to (once a
Great Umpire, sob). There used to be a nice old

gin-soaked Great-Granny. When she went to the Great Throne in the Sky you couldn't read about anything else for weeks.

Then there's Granny (the Queen) who is V. Nice to dogs and horses and is married to a Greek with his foot in his mouth. The Kiddies include the Hair Apparent, whose hair is not very apparent and who is getting V. Depressed because he should be King by now but his mother won't abdicate.

Prince Charles is a thoughtful cove which makes him V. Unpopular with the Gutter Press who think he is a Wimp, Communist, Etck. His ex-wife Diana sold more magazines than anyone in history and was therefore seen to be a Good Thing. When she died the PM went on about the People's Princess and everyone got all weepy as if they had known her personally. And all the papers said END OF THE MONARCHY etck. But as El Chubb predicted, just as many old folks turned out for the Queen mum's funeral, so I think the old royals will be with us a bit longer . . .

There are lots of royal family bit parts but I feel sorry for old Camilla Parker B, who is always written about like she's the back end of three buses. Other Royal Firm members include Fergie, the flame-haired temptress, and various UNCLES IN NAVY, looking for jobs etck.

NB. American teenage worriers have one dream: to marry Harry. I feel a song coming on. Or possibly a divorce.

You have to get divorced or separated to be a fully paid-up member of the Royal Firm today, unless you are the head. But it is a V. Good Thing that as a result of this humble little alphabet the Queen now pays taxes. Here's what I wrote:

'*But it is V. Worrying that the Richest Woman in the World does not pay any Taxes. Surely if she did we could all pay less? Teenage Worriers everywhere, write to Queenie and ask her why. Maybe we could publish her answers and make a mint (I mean enlighten the World as to her V. Good reasons for not shelling out. Hah!).*'

And now she does! Thanks to Teenage Worriers everywhere.

SCHOOL

Yeek. At least my parents don't pay for me to be bored stiff for six hours a day five days a week like Hazel's do. I get bored for free.

When you think about it, it is V. Odd to coop up healthy Vital (ho ho) youngsters with a handful of exasperated adults and even fewer books when they could all be hiking over green fields, rummaging through skips, writing poems, inventing Spot cures, Etck.

THE BIG WORRIES ABOUT SCHOOL ARE BULLIES AND EXAMS.

Bullies are worst in the whimsically named playground, and I would ban school breaks so we could either go home half an hour earlier or spend time in the library or nice comfy rooms with couches and TV. How many adults would like to be flung into an Asphalt Jungle with a group of thugs and no shops, pubs, betting shops, Etck to go to?

People also hate Uniforms but I wish Sluggs had one and then every day wouldn't cause a serious outbreak of Fashion Worry about who has the best trainers. Hazel says St Mary's Academy is just as bad though, because although they all have to

Rover, unaffected by Exam Worry

attire themselves (that's how their Headteacher talks) in flattering bottle green (wince, writhe), there are loads of different ways of WEARING it (ie you can have a long jumper outside your skirt or a sleeveless short one tucked in, Etck Etck).

DOWN WITH PRIVATE SCHOOLS! STOP ETON BEING A CHARITY, etck. (Private schools, skittishly called Public Schools, have charitable Status. In Case You Didn't Know this Terrible Fact, you will not be reading it in a Newspaper Near You.) I take this somewhat strident view even though I am a gentle freedom-loving soul, who believes everyone has the right to choose, BECAUSE, if Private Schools were BANNED, then all the nice well-educated rich folk would get V. Bossy with the other schools so their darlings wld learn to spell, etck and everyone would benefit. Instead of jumble sales for a few extra measly quid to repaint the concrete dinosaur that no one plays on, we would have Classical Music Concerts raising millions and everyone would have a fully working felt-tip pen.

> **TIP:** If you are being bullied, make sure everyone knows about it. I know this is easier said than done but when I eventually persuaded my parents and the teachers to take me seriously, I ended up feeling Quite Sorry for the bully, as everyone hated her. (Since then, she has become quite human and Aggy and I no longer skulk about in terror.)

SEX

I hope you haven't turned to this page first because
as in all great works (ahem) each subject should
be seen in a deep and meaningful context and,
as you know, Sex is something that should only
take place in a warm and supportive bed, I mean
relationship, where both partners like and respect
each other.

Sex is usually taken to mean sexual intercourse
but the good sort (so I am told ahem) always
includes Foreplay, which some people say means
the Boy takes his socks off, but which should
include: kissing each other's Bits all over, various
fondling and indeed even V.V. Exciting things
like Holding Hands, eg Holding the hand of One
You Really Lurve produces URGES much stronger
than a full-blown snog with Sid Crotch from Year
9.

Sex is one of those things everybody talks about
a lot but V. Few people actually do much of. This
is because when they have worked and eaten and
slept there is not much time. Given that it is supposed to be the most fun you can have without
paying, this seems odd, but who am I to say? The
average number of times married couples Do It is
about twice a week! Maybe unmarried couples Do
It more often.

When I am an adult couple I am sure I will
do it twice a night at least, which will play havoc

with the National Average. NB: The Nat Av is
probably much lower as this is not a subject
people are honest about and unless you had a Sex-
Spy in every bedroom, bush, multi-storey carpark,
broom cupboard, loo, garden shed, Etck it would
be hard to assess the TRUE RATE of British
Nookie.

However, when you have never Done It at all
(like Moi) it is a Worry. Firstly because you are not
sure whether everyone else is as experienced as they
SAY they are and secondly, when you try to get real

details from your friends they go COY. (Even Hazel, who started Doing It with her cousin when he was 14 and she was 13 – yeech, they could have got ARRESTED – and hasn't stopped since, has never gone into graphic detail.)

On the other end of the scale is Aggy, who has never held hands, even with gloves on.

Boys gets V. Worried too, and are sometimes relieved if they find a Girl has never Done It, because then she won't be able to compare Willies, Etck. Maybe this is why so many thickos call girls slags if they have Done It.

Rover has no concept of virginity

LETTY CHUBB'S TAKE THE WORRY OUT OF SEX CAMPAIGN

Every Teenager Worrier over 16 to be taught about Sex by a fully qualified, V. Handsome, person of their choice in V. Sumptuous, V. Private surroundings (saunas, satin couches, palm trees, etck). Lessons to be taken at own pace (ie courses could last five mins or three years depending how shy you were). They would include maps on How to Find Your Erogenous Zones and Make the Most of Them as well as all the boring technical stuff you get anyway about How Not to Have Babies, etck. Falling in Lurve with your tutor would be an occupational hazard but since this happens anyway when they are old and hairy and MARRIED it couldn't be any worse.

An even better alternative would be for Virgins to discover about it together. It would be much less intimidating, even if you did put everything in the wrong place. Yes! Lose your virginity in PAIRS. (As long as you are over 16, preferably about 22, and wearing cap, condom, etck.)

Course, I know the best thing of all is to be Eternally in Lurve (when it all comes naturally) like Granny and Granpa Chubb were (sob). See also WILLIES etck etck.

SKIN

Flimsy stuff that holds you together. I used to be V. worried about cutting myself in case I fell out, but Age and the Playground has cured me of this. Now the big Worry is what your skin looks like. My mother is V. Unsympathetic and says wait till you get wrinkles and saggy bits then you'll know what Worry really is.

It is weird no one has invented synthetic skin you can just stretch over yourself for special dates, but I expect Aggy will soon, then I can market it and give her a cut (heh! heh!). See also ACNE and COSMETICS.

Even dewy Teenettes in the bloom of Yoof can get nose-to-mouth lines. **CHUBB TIP:** Sleep with sticky-tape over them. Hey Presto! They are gone! (By lunch time they are back.)

SMOKING

Why oh why do my parents do it? I am V.
Ashamed, especially as they should know better
and if they saved the money we could have holidays
abroad, savings accounts, nest eggs we could give
Boyz for breakfast, Etck. I will be V. Upset if they
pop their socks prematurely but they will get no
sympathy.

Aggy has started smoking the occasional fag
and is V. Distraught about it because she is too
intelligent to smoke, she thinks. I agree, even
though she does have real problems what with
her mother and the postman and five siblings. Once
you start, it is V. Hard to stop, but if you want to
Smell, Spend a Fortune and Die Young it's your
business. I have no wish to interfere with Freedom
of Choice but when I am in the Govt I will just
put fags up to a million pounds a pack, and
provide free transport so the toiling masses can
have fun without smoking. Funding for this simple
project will be provided by the many and fertile
ideas of the Teenage Think Tank (ahem, blush).

COUGH Splutter

SOAP OPERAS

I'm not sure why they're called Soap Operas. I can
understand the Opera part, because they go on a

long time, everybody exaggerates the smallest little setbacks like somebody losing their handkerchief or something, and you can't understand what's going on.

The thing about Soaps is not getting HOOKED. If you fall in love with someone in a Soap, you go mad, hanging about outside telly studios, writing them letters they reply to with a photo with their signature printed on it, thinking they're the person they play in the show, and all for somebody who lies under his car all day and calls Girls birds. If you are hooked on somebody in a Soap you can read a new terrible Thing about him in the papers every day, like he goes out with three Golden-Haired Lovelies all at the same time, but none of the four million people reading about it should tell his wife because it's only a bit of fun.

SOCCER

Football (sob, yearn, missed opps, Etck) is only called soccer by people from posh schools who think it's played with the wrong-shaped ball. All you need to know is that whichever side kicks it into the net most times wins, which they do by holding the shirts and kicking the ankles of the other lot (how different it might have been if the likes of Moi had been flying up the field, sob, bitterness, spleen, Etck). Anyway, most Boyz spend Saturday morning playing it, Saturday afternoon watching it, Saturday evening (and others) talking about it Very Loudly and Sunday slumped in front of the telly watching the game they just watched yesterday.

My experience of being banned from exercising my Agility, Grace and Demonic Ball-Weaving Skills have made me somewhat cynical but it is a drag that Boyz will react to football by doing all the things you hoped they'd do for you: spend a fortune, burst into tears when things Go Wrong, Remember Every Little Moment However Trivial, Dress Up, Never Forget a Date, Etck Etck. Pah!

SPERM

Sperm is white gooey stuff that comes out of Boyz' willies (so I am told, ahem) and from what you hear about how much pressure keeping it in puts boys under it's a surprise to me they don't keep exploding like balloons and we aren't all permanently covered in it. Very Moral People and some Feminists would say that the reason boyz are so keen to squirt sperm all over the place is that they've been brought up to see Girls as Sex Objects

Sperm; magnified 50 zillion times

who are very anxious to receive lots of it. There may be some truth in this, but since sperm contains the little swimming things that fertilize the eggs inside girls and therefore make sure there are enough human beings to go round, I suppose it's only to be expected that it will try to carry out its Mission whenever possible, or rather its Emission, ha ha yeech.

It seems to be just as well that sperms don't communicate with each other because if they ever heard from their ancestors they wouldn't bother to come out at all, since Boyz seem to spend a lot of time squirting them on loo walls, pictures of computer programmers from Basildon with no tops on, and all over their boxer shorts. Even if the boy is doing what the little spermlets hope he's doing, they're likely to come hurtling out, yelling and waving their tails only to charge splat into a giant rubber bag, which must make them wonder if it was all worth it. However, don't feel sorry for them, because a condom bothers them a lot less than they will bother you unless you want to hear the patter of tiny feet, Etck.

Boys secretly Worry about sperm, like everything else to do with their Willies. They Worry about it coming out when it's not supposed to (like when they're in church, or on the bus, or being examined by the doctor, or standing in front of the class reading Shakespeare – none of these things is likely, but when did that stop anybody Worrying?) or they Worry about it coming out too soon when they're with the Girl of Their Dreams, like before the Girl is at the Height of Passion or maybe before they've even got their trousers off. They also Worry about it not having enough swimming things in it to make them fathers, in which case they think they won't be admitted as a real man and get clapped on the back and told they've got a lot of lead in their pencils, Etck Etck.

That's enough about Sperm for now, especially from someone who's never seen any, honest.

STRIKES

To have a Strike, you have to have a Union, 'cos if it's just You, no one takes any notice, or else they go out and get someone else to do the job. I wld like to be a Great Labour Leader and march at the head of a cheering throng carrying banners but it is more likely I will make V. Good Historical Films about it, to show people what it was like when Humble Workers had Rights and a 40 hour week (instead of working 80 hours or no hours like today).

SUPERSTITION

My next book is going to be called *I'm Not Superstitious, Touch Wood*. Order now as there will be a huge demand. My only superstitions just now are the usual ones (Ladders, Magpies, Black Cats, Friday the 13th, Spilling the Salt, Cracks in the Pavement, Not Wearing Green Socks etck) but I have a few v. special ones of my own like avoiding odd numbers (see HABITS), avoiding any use of the word about dying that rhymes with 'breath' – as you know, I always use 'banana' here, but I also use that for my figure which is v. confusing and makes me wonder if analysis would be worth the money after all – and not going out on Wednesday nights.

Superstitious Teenettes, afflicted with Number-worry,
welcoming the advent of Teenage years with unalloyed Joy

TIP: If Superstition Worry is debilitating you, notice
how many old people there are who are not
superstitious. And they are still alive after YEARS of
not Worrying about magpies, Etck so take cheer.

CHAPTER ELEVEN
(TUVW)

No reply from DH but I am seeing him tomorrow
(yipppeeeee, swoon, white Christmas! Hearts,
flowers, etck etck).

I am V. Worried about my father. I found an
empty bottle of whisky in his desk drawer along
with four different sets of bath taps. He just can't
seem to get any that fit. We are all beginning to
smell. I put back the bits of his Great Work I had
been reading and found some new stuff.

I would go to Aggy's but there are so many kids
and Hazel's Mum has not been too welcoming
since the Party. Apparently you just can't get
red jelly out of bath towels. It takes ages to
wash in the sink. (Us, not the towels.) Benjy is
V.V. Happy about it though. Today he read his
first whole sentence: 'The cat sat on the mat.'
My mother is delighted and says it's all the
work she's been doing with phonetics, whatever
that is.

Sadly, the next night he dreamt the mat ate Rover.

My father is trying to get BT to put in a phone
for Granny Chubb. She can't go to the phone box
any more since the day she found a crate of three

basking sharks in there. I hope she is not losing her remaining marbles.

There is a lot of washing-up to do. It's a pity my father couldn't have chosen the kitchen taps for his experiment. Horace just goes round on his wheel as normal. He has no feelings. However, I fear he may put in an appearance in my father's book soon.

I am seeing Daniel tomorrow! Have been listening to John Cage all week but found 'four minutes and 32 seconds' a little baffling. Must think of interesting things to say about the quality of silence. Or maybe something wrong with my CD? I have also tried to read Proust, who DH raves about, but I keep getting stuck on the biscuit. It reminds me of my aunt who used to worry about plain biscuits feeling LONELY if you took the fancy ones. Also spent three months pocket money on new trainers, piercing my ears and a hairdo. It is great, v. short and spiky. I have had detention every day for a week for daydreaming.

TEACHERS

If you are V. Polite and Smarmy to Teachers they will swiftly assume you are V.V. Clever, which leads to good marks for coursework and you

Teachers I have known

might pass your exams just on this. Also, write everything out V. Tidily (hard for Moi, whose scripts resemble a Daddy Longlegs mating with a Hippo) and even if you have copied it straight out of the WH Smith crib-books they will still say 'Excellent work', and everything will be fine until Twenty years later when the Nation goes bankrupt, doctors ask each other what an appendix is, the PM has to keep leaving No. 10 to go on courses in Japan, Etck.

The most important Teacher is the Head. Ours is Mr Hesseltine and he likes to think he rules with a Rod of Iron but that, although Tough, is Tender too. He is v. keen to have you think he understands the Joy and Pain of Yoof, Etck but he looks V. Foolish in jeans and a pink shirt and since the appearance of an unkind portrait of him in the girls' lavvy (not by me, honest) he has had the sense to realize this. I do not like to think of him in the girls' lavvy but apart from his habit of gargling in wet cement while quoting the Dalai Lama he is not as Bad as Some, eg the Deputy Head, Miss Farthing. (Perhaps her name explains why she looks down on those of us who drop our 'h's. Hah!)

Miss Farthing was roped in to try and stuff as many pupils through GCSEs as possible (after Sluggs came third worst in Inner London's *Horror Schools Exposé* in 1999). Since then it has improved dramatically but at what cost? Farthing's first move was to change the intake (this is like when the Govt change the voting boundaries so they get more seats even when fewer people vote for them) and now one quarter of Sluggs is Middle Class (nearly). Her next move was to avoid any contact with Slobs, Truants and Thickies so all of them got placed in Broadmoor, Remand Homes, the SAS, Police Cadet School, Etck. Currently, she is banning any fun. She has never had any herself so why should anyone else?

TIP: Teachers come in easy-to-spot types. $\frac{0}{10}$

NOT-SO-YOUNG-BUT-V. KEEN-TO-BE-TRENDY: Pink shirts, jeans, optional medallion (yeech). V. Keen to talk about 'pop music' and 'sex-uality' rather than teach. Always asking if you need to tell them something about what is really trou-bling your SOUL. V. Easy to get sent home sick by these ones, esp with Girls' probs.

POLITICAL: Purple or red jumpsuits. Badges. Men have long hair, women have short spiky hair. Great fun, as if you mention Oppression or Sexism they get V.V. Interested in you and a lesson is whiled peacefully away chatting about how V. Unfair the world is.

ARTY: Long skirts with flowers on or flares (glug). Best fun of all as V. Involved in your Creative Potential eg a decorative doodle on the margin, especially if abstract, can absorb more attention than the not V. Good spelling opposite.

DEEP: Too busy thinking to care how they look and so often more interesting to behold than anything at the zoo. An example would be tartan trousers, slippers, a roll-neck jumper and pearls plus pac-a-mac. Usually V. nice and vague. Doodle as above and try to insert FREUDIAN OVERTONES. Also, if lesson getting sticky, mention the Space-Time Continuum or how V. Interesting is a grain of sand. They do not notice if you are asleep.

HEARTY: Tweeds or shorts. Do not mention the Space-Time Continuum. They make you work V. Fast, no nonsense, spell-it-right-get-out-for-a-breath-of-fresh-air-stop-horsing-around- work-is-work-and-play-is-play-etck. As long as you write a lot and don't waste time thinking about anything they are Quite Easy. They have a V. Cheery smile whatever has happened and if we all fail our GCSEs because we have not understood any of the questions they are not downhearted. 'On with the next lot' they cry fearlessly and live to fight another day, Etck.

SCIENTIFIC: Glasses, do not tuck in their shirts. Not many of these boffins left at Inner

City comprehensives but V. Good if you want to piddle about making paper aeroplanes as they get V. Excited about aerodynamics, harnessing Free Energy, Saving the Planet, etck. V. Inspiring like most endangered species.

GULLIBLE: These are Supply and New teachers so if you all hum softly in unison they always think it's the radiator and you can miss a whole lesson while they try to get the heating fixed. They also sit on farting cushions, etck without getting cross.

LITERARY: This type is always V. Spindly (don't ask me why) and Worried-looking even though they take solace in the well-honed phrase. I like this lot best as they understand the Deep and Festering Worries of the Creative Soul. If you use enough adjectives and alliteration and write about V. Deep subjects like the Last Pit Pony they will be over the moon, even if they are teaching Biology at the time.

NB. Sucking up to teachers is an ART. First, no one (especially the teacher, hah!) must know you are doing it. Also, once you have mastered it (cheerful smile for Hearty, Anguished look for Trendy, etck etck) you can get away with Murder. You will never be the one they think of when someone has sprayed Fart-Spray all round the staff room.

TELEVISION

Does it rot the brain? If Shakespeare had had a telly no doubt he would have written fewer plays, but he would have made more money doing *Eastenders*, Etck so who is the loser? Just because the people making telly progs all have brain rot it doesn't mean we ALL do. TV after 9pm is best and Kids TV is worst. All the presenters speak like Minnie Mouse (or else shout at 10 mill. decibels) and dress up like Toddlers which any self-respecting six-year-old finds pukesome. But since my adored and revered Mater and Pater are the only parents in London who have not forked out for a DVD player yet (and as our video has been broken for about a year now, moan, wail Etck), we have to make do with watching everything that's on.

I used to write in for tickets for *Top of the Pops*, Etck and get crushes on Soap Stars but now I am more Interested in Real Life eg I get free eye checks while I can and Worry about TV Irradiation and daydream.

See also SOAP OPERAS.

THIRD WORLD DEBT

V.V.V.V. big Worry. This is what the POOR countries in the world owe to all the RICH countries in

Circle the person who most needs . . .

the world (like us – I know, I know, but you should
see some of the others). We and America lent all
these poor countries money and now they can't
afford to pay the interest. This means that instead
of using their crops to feed their own people they
are selling them to try to repay us. And they
NEVER WILL BE ABLE TO.

It is V. Peculiar that banks can let Big Business
have tons of money and never get it back when
they are asking the parents of starving babies to
pay up by yesterday.

Once you start to Worry about this, it is V.
Difficult to justify Worrying about anything else.

So maybe the best thing to do would be just to Worry about the Third World Debt until it is SOLVED.

I will get the Teenage Think Tank to do this first.

TIME

Time has always been here and always will be here. It will go on for the whole of the future and yet there is never enough of it. If that does not Worry you, then you are CURED.

However, if you do not know what to DO with Time and feel it slipping through your fingers or stretching endlessly before you like a desolate wasteland (where have I heard that phrase before?) then turn on the telly and before you know it three whole hours will have passed. This is what is V. Scary about time, because however much you try to control it by parcelling it up into minutes and seconds and however much you try to FILL it by having meals, examining your Spots, sitting on the loo, Etck, it still leaps, crawls, hurtles or drags by in a V. Whimsical fashion. Just try making it go V. Fast when you are at the Dentist or V. Slowly when you are with the Person of your Dreams and you will see what I mean.

Also, could Time ever Stop? Although this

**Members of the Teenage Think Tank will have to address
such questions as: What If Time Stops?**

thought makes your brain hurt it is good exercise
and is the kind of daily thing you will have to
think about to qualify for the Teenage Think Tank.

TODDLERS

Dwarfish bipeds who are screaming for sweeties in
the newsagents while you're queuing for *Tru-Luv,
Smirk*, etck. Quite often their pet adult will be
saying no but sooner or later they will say yes and
all will be quiet for a few seconds except for the
newsagent muttering 'If it was mine I'd belt it.'
Remember Toddlers are what ickle wincy Babies
grow into, V. Fast. Be warned.

TONGUE

What doctors are supposed to look at to see if you are well but they never do. This leaves Yoof free to indulge in daily Tongue-Worry, ie Is it wearing six fur jackets and if so does it mean terminal Illness or a Sniffle? Also used for French-kissing (which can be mastered, they say, regardless of Nationality, but I haven't got the hang of it yet) and for tasting food. If eating something you don't like, it is V. Hard to avoid touching it with your tongue.

TRANSPORT

The car is now the only form of transport that the Govt likes. However, it is still possible to spot the quaint old-fashioned double-decker-style red Bus, which forages in small packs many miles apart in some of our great Cities and at the rate things are going will probably soon be drawn by horses again, or teams of unemployed people. Although `Red' Ken Livingstone, mayor of London, has improved ye buses of late, catching buses is still an Art and it is V. Frustrating that when you have succeeded you still have to get off at your stop and let it go till next time. If we had been this kind to the Buffalo the world might be a better place.

Londoners are also V. Lucky to have the splendid

Transportation
is no trouble
to fleas

Rover is untroubled by Transport Worry

Tube train in which you can get V. Cosy with a lot
of strangers in the pitch dark. Despite making it
V. Hard to get into and out of the tube stations
because of a lot of barriers that eat your ticket but
still don't open, tubes seem V. Popular, especially in
the Rush Hour, when everything does the opposite
of rushing. Luckily stations did not have barriers
when the last big tube fire happened. I hope they
will take them down before the next one. There are
also escalators at tube stations and these sometimes
work but usually tube travel involves a lot of tiring
going up stairs so I would rather hunt for a bus (or
maybe they are hunting us, after all, but just aren't
v. good at it).

Railway trains and big lorries are the other
forms of transport. The lorries are called coaches
when they are used for people and travel V. Fast
without safety belts, tsk, but are V. Cheap and
Cheerful unlike the trains.

**The Teenage Think Tank will have solved Transport
Worry by the Year 3000**

TIP: If you are brave enough to cycle (unlike Moi) it is the most reliable form of avoiding Transport-Worry. Still, you need a helmet, plus an anti-tank gun for blasting motorists before they get you, and blowing off the doors they open as you are sailing by. Also fluorescent stripes, knee pads, etck. Also V. Good bolts and chains and huge bag for pump, lights, and wheels which get removed if you park your bike for 2 secs.

TRAVEL

Broadens the Mind. It is amazing to think there are all those sunlit beaches, waterfalls, deserts, rain-forests, mountains, Etck that I could be cavorting in with Daniel if only I had the money and the courage to fly to them. They are there all the time, even when you are missing your bus (or your boyfriend) on a drizzly pavement.

I am hoping that someone will invent thought travel by the time I am 18, so that you can just think of a place and be there. England would get V. Empty of course.

UNIVERSITY

Everybody says anyone with half a brain should go to University if they can. This is a way of achieving

Lo! Who is that Ravishing Damsel? So Beautiful yet so Learnéd?

And is there Honey still for Tea?

your Potential, getting a Good Job, Etck. Sad to say, although they are stuffing lots more students in so that the Centres of Excellence are now bursting at the seams and they have to do lectures in shifts, it is increasingly hard for said students to keep body and soul together. Everyone owes a fortune before they start and unless you are lucky enough to be the son or daughter of the Prince of W., you spend most of your blissful Days of Enlightenment wrapped in fifteen layers of clothing and living in basements (where at least you can grow free mushrooms).

Of course the posh Univs with Dreaming Spires sound V. Pleasant. I would V. Much like to waft around a sunlit sward spouting poetry and punting from cream teas to crumpets like Ashley, but the chances of getting to Oxbridge from Sluggs are zillions to one and Aggy is that One.

TIP: Since the once Great British Umpire has contracted and we are now worse educated than weeny places like Portugal, it is worth trying to get as much education as you can to compete with Euro whizz-kids. (Even if most billionaires do seem to have left school at the earliest opportunity. NB: If you have a Business Talent, send me your ideas NOW.) FE colleges, Art Schools, Drama Schools, etck are easier options than Univ. You need V. Little talent for some of them (look at My Mother . . .). Since it is so V. Worrying considering a CAREER, Univ or something like it can help you put off the Worry. Maybe there will be more good jobs by the time you are out! And it will be V. Good for the unemployment figs and Crime rate (as the Govt knows only too well).

UTOPIA

Opposite of what we've got now. When the Teenage Think Tank runs the country we will have it. V. Worrying to think of those squillions of people who never lived to see it.

VAGINA

The bit of a Girl that babies come out of (usually after a Willy has been either in or V. Near it). Also where you get your Periods from, and also slippery fluids, espesh when you feel Urges. But if you are a Girl, what do you call it? AND what do you call the bit you pee out of? Boys have it V. Easy here. One bit of them performs both functions and is cosily called the Willy. But girls are forced to put up with V. Coy phrases like 'Down There' or 'Under Bits'. 'Pussy' is not only rude but V. Odd if you have a cat and 'FANNY' is American for Bum. Suggestions welcome.

NB. There is also not a cosy name for the clitoris which is the little bit at the front which I am told gives you all the fun (ahem) and gets V. Excited

Rover does not worry about what to call her Naughty Bits

under pressure (like the Willy). This is where big Urges come from, but it is thought to be even ruder to mention it than the Willy, so lots of Girls do not know much about it. (Unfair, whinge, sexism.) Not that I would like to have parents who talked about things like this OPENLY, like Hazel's next-door neighbours, the Plunket-Breezes. They are always breezing off to Nudist Beaches. No wonder the Junior Plunket-Breezes have left home to work in commerce.

> **TIP:** Although Girls worry more about their Buzooms than their Vaginas, there are some who think: is it too small? Or too big? Since they are V. Elastic this should be classed as a V. Minor Worry, even by L. Chubb.

VAMPIRES

I have just read that in the USA there are FIVE HUNDRED people who classify themselves as *Blood-sucking Vampires*. This is another V. Good reason not to travel far.

VOICE

V. Worrying for boys about 14 which is when it

Sadly, there is no way to fix a Breaking Voice

starts to break and then they sound like shrimps hiccuping. This is perfectly normal, Hah! And unless you are earning a fortune as a Choir Boy, nothing to Worry about. But voices can be Worrying for girls too, as deep voices are more popular than high ones which is why Politicians and Newscasters Etck go for elocution and voice-training lessons. And who has the deepest voices? Why, Boyz, of course. UP WITH SQUEAKY VOICES.

Also, in the New Classless Society (ho ho) it still counts to speak BBC English. Pah!

WAR

Always going on somewhere. This should be the main thing for the TTT (Teenage Think Tank) to address. Otherwise, if there are still wars in fifty years time, it will be OUR fault. Teenage Worriers of the World, the future is in our hands. NB. Just getting their strongest person to fight our strongest person (thank you, Benjy) won't work. See also KILLING and PACIFISM.

WATER

Twenty years ago, my mother says, when you went Abroad, you Never Drank the Water. Now, Abroad is the only place the Middle Classes ever do drink it. In their own backyard, they use filters or bottled stuff. Also, it is no longer Free. It is a tragedy that

It may only be a drop in the ocean now... but what about fish suppers in the 21st century?

Stone Age Worrier

Young People Like Moi, who have never even peed in the sea, are forced to add yet another Worry to the ever-increasing list of Twenty-first Century Angst.

END THIS WATER CARNAGE NOW

In a V. Rare case of controlling my Worry, I am Banning V. Expensive, Silly Mineral Water. If we all DIE of water poisoning the Govt will be V. Sorry, but at least they would clean up the water. Drink water straight from the TAP, even if you ARE middle class. It is the STAFF OF LIFE (or is that doughnuts . . .?). If I can do it, so can you (yeech). Maybe I'll give it a quick boil first.

WEATHER

The only month I feel v. good about is Sept. It is usually still quite Warm but not too hot and it is post the Hay Fever season. Also, one or two leafy green things are still waving cheerfully. All Winter I cough and sneeze because of the cold and all Summer I cough and sneeze because of my allergies. My mother is always nagging me about wrapping up warm and keeping dry but even a V. Worried Spindly Weed like Moi is hardly likely to be seen DEAD with an umbrella at my age. Ditto rain hats, wellies, Etck. And the

Snowman bobble Hat Granny Chubb knitted me, though V. Sweet, is something I would only consider putting on at Granny Chubb's doorstep after a secret-agent-style check that I haven't been followed.

Emigration to a silver beach in a mosquito-free zone is the only answer once I have got V. Rich and completed the 'Conquer-Your-Fear-Of-Flying-In-Two-Hundred-Easy-Stages' course I have just sent off for.

> **TIP:** Cure your Climate-Worries by sending me £50 towards development costs of the Letty Chubb Climate Control Bubble. And with the proceeds I shall control the climate by emigrating to a far off Sunny Isle. Hah!

WEDDINGS

Ever seen a stick insect in tulle? I will never be a Bridesmaid ever ever again. And my experience is a V. Bad Omen for my own Marriage, should I ever be daft enough to succumb to a Proposal (chance would be a fine thing). I confess I occasionally have a sneaky feeling that I would like it if my own parents had had the Grace to get Married. V. Conventional of me, I know, but that's how we Worriers are. Bright side is, they can't get a Divorce. Hah!

TIP: If you are worried that you will never walk Up the Aisle with the Person of your Dreams, think of how many People walked straight back down again. I have often pondered that people should say `Do I?' instead of 'I Do' and one of my first V. Important Experimental Films will be to run a Wedding Sequence backwards and make a V. Serious and Deep Point. Also, Weddings are V. Expensive. You could have several Honeymoons instead (with several partners, hah!). Or give the loot to Charity (guilt, lash).

I will never be a bridesmaid ever ever again

WILLIES

Like buzooms, Willies come in many different shapes and sizes, all of them perfectly NORMAL. But as we have seen above, being perfectly Normal is not V. Comforting and I am sorry to have to say it, but most boys Worry about their Willies more than about the State of the Universe, War, Peace, Etck.

Worriers should know that the Willy-Dormant bears little relationship to the Willy-Rampant when it comes to SIZE, so all those meanies who mock their mates in the loo had better wait till they've seen the Willy-Rampant.

Also, Willies can be V. Shy, so that although yours may have been skittish on the bus, at tea at your Auntie's and all Night Long when you have no one to share it with except your Mum's newly-washed sheets, you may find it abandoning you

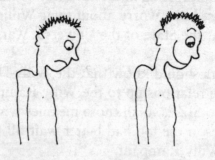

The Willy dormant   **The Willy rampant**

just when Sandra, for whom you have Yearned, runs a playful finger up your leg.

As a sister, I have so far only seen two Willies-Dormant, but I have seen a lot of tight trousers (MORE LEVI 501 ads NOW) and I have a good imagination. I am V.V.V. Lucky (and the only Girl I know), not to have seen a Flasher. It is V. Unfair that you are not allowed to see pictures of Willies-Rampant when you can see Women's Bits all over the Newsagents. Personally, I would rather see neither, but it is a V. Sordid World in which Flashers roam the streets frightening the life out of people whereas you're not allowed to see pictures which would be a matter of Choice.

(This is clearly an indication of Letty's protected life. Her eyes have not yet roamed to the top shelves where Playgirl perches – Ed.)

For more on Willy-Worries, see EJACULATION, ERECTION and SPERM and SEX.

Etck. Etck.
Etck.

I am too sad to draw
lots of pictures of
different types of
willy here. V. sorry.
Read on (SOB) to
see why.....

CHAPTER TWELVE (XYZ)

This has been the worst week of my life ever. It is hard to write. The words just seem to slip between my fingers. I went to the river, but Daniel didn't come. After four hours I went round to his house and saw Hazel coming out. I couldn't believe it. I hit her. She was amazed. Then she recognized me (I'd forgotten about my hairdo). She was round there looking for her BROTHER, she SAID. (Ha!)

I phoned Aggy in despair and her father said she was round at some boy's house. (AGGY????) He gave me the number.

It was Daniel's.

Well, obviously he had meant to meet me somewhere else and phoned her in despair because I wasn't there.

But no. I went round and Daniel wouldn't let me in. Then he recognized me and admitted all. Last time I saw him he had met Aggy coming out of my house in tears (the babysitting night! Arghhh). He had walked her home, to be kind, and then found that she was so vulnerable, so alone, so brilliant and sensitive and . . . I expect you will be puking by now. I certainly was. To cap it all, he said he thought my alphabet was 'Immature'.

Arghhh! I rushed home to burn it, but I cried so much the matches wouldn't catch.

My mother came in and was really really kind. It is the first time we have talked for about a year. And she is the reason that this alphabet is coming to you now. Thank God it's nearly finished.

I have written to the Archbishop of Canterbury for advice about being a nun and serving the community.

Goodbye Hope, adieu childish things, I shall apply myself to Good Deeds, Noble Thoughts and the Third World Debt. But I will never ever forgive sensitive, vulnerable, treacherous Aggy as long as I live.

I am writing this only to save my parents from a fate worse than banana.

If this alphabet gives you the impression of jollity it will only be because I am smiling through my tears.

Given that my life is now dust and ashes and that all my hopes are sunk to the bottom of the sea it is just as well I do not have to Worry about:

XYLOPHONES

Instruments that sound like milk bottles being hit with slippers.

XXX

To me, XXX used to mean Kisses. As a Nun, I will probably only kiss the smooth brows of infants whose Mothers have abandoned them and who I will take in and nurture (when I am not in the Nuns' film school labouring over Religious Documentaries and broadening my Mind).

YOUTH

Gone, all gone. I trust the World will be a better place for Benjy than it has proved to be for me.

ZODIAC

I try hard not to be Bitter, but Aggy is an Aries, the sign that Sagittarius (the Treacherous Daniel) always opts for. Hitler was an Aries, too. I give you Letty Chubb's Zodiac . . . I am too weary to write more . . . Adieu.

FINAL CHAPTER

Funny old world.

It is now six whole weeks since that Terrible Day ... and I have pieced together the fragments of my desolate etck etck, despite having no reply so far from the archbish.

Hazel took me riding every day for a week after the Tragic Day, even though she has a black eye. She finally told me she has been seeing a GIRL and KISSING HER!!!!!

I was gobsmacked. There will be a lot of boys gnashing their teeth and hurling themselves off tower blocks when the news gets Out.

Aggy gave Benjy a kitten for Christmas, so I am sneezing more. She also wrote a V. Long letter apologizing. She said when Love Comes So Strong, Etck Etck. I didn't realize she had been eating her heart out for Daniel since before I'd even met him ... anyway, she's much cleverer than him so it won't last.

I let her writhe in agony for a few days ... but we are Frendz again.

My mother has been offered a contract to design wallpaper! It turns out she'd been painting designs into the night at a friend's STUDIO, because she thought if she did it at home My Father would say she was Wasting Her Time.

I didn't realize how much I had been Worrying about this.

My mother is obviously the best chance we have of beating the bailiff. My father's Great Work, as far as I can see, has turned into the Man living in the Log Cabin with a whole Menagerie of animals he communicates Ancient Wisdom with, and they are planning to take over the Government when the Great Crisis comes and brings forth a New Age. My Father has obviously become loonier than Mad Mikey Jackson, but I think he's harmless.

My photos got fifth prize in a local newspaper competition. The editor said they had 'depth'. I won six rolls of film.

Brian sent me a box of chocolates and a poem for Christmas. It was rather good. I have noticed he has new specs and his complexion is much better . . .

I am still Worried. I would like to say I wasn't but my main worries just now are my stoop, my GCSEs, my hair (which I really HATE . . . it's all spiky), and the way my face moves about when I talk. I have only just noticed this, because normally you don't see yourself talking. I wish I'd never done the video course.

I am not Worried about Daniel any more. His hair isn't like wet sand at sunset, more like rubber bands. 'Endless desolate wasteland.' Ha!

The End
-
(Nearly)

Since I got my wig cut.
Even More stray Bits
(get more gel) =

OZONE
(High worry level - don't look up)

still just
Mole (hidden by fringe, check daily for changes)

Freckles
(come and go)

Spots
(Still come and goo)

Pointy Nose
(but the NUNS won't mind)

Cold Sore
(for 3-4 months of year only)

Round Shoulders
(must take up Yoga)

Brazone (still use magnifying glass, sob)

Granny Chubb's Jumper
(knitted when I was ten)

Hands in Pockets

School Bag
(contains same stuff + copy of "NUNS - Have you got a VOCATION")

Stick-insect zone
(Eat more PLUMPO)

Flat Foot

Glass ankles
V. fragile. Don't work on roller skates.

V. Expensive Trainers. But why do they look better on Fred Kool?

Me. Moi. Myself.
Striding towards a new dawn.....

L. Chubb's 'Teenage-Worriers' Questionnaire.... ♥ ♥

Fill it in if you feel like it! (For my next book, he he.)
It is Anonymous (so no-one will know who you are!)

Age: Sex:.

LOOKS: What do you dislike most about your appearance?

• What do you like most?

SCHOOL: Do you go to Private ☐, State ☐ Church/State ☐. What do you like most about school?

• What do you dislike most?

• What subjects will you take (if any) for GCSEs?

• Will you stay on after 16 ☐ do any Further Education? ☐

FAMILY: Are your parents together? ☐ If so, are they married?   If living with one parent, which one?   And do you see the other?   Give ages of siblings   Do you get on with your brothers/sisters?   If you don't have any, would you like some?
Do you have a pet?   What pet would you like to have?

INTERESTS: Name them!

JOBS: What would you most like to do?
What job are you most likely
to get?

FRIENDS: Do you have a best friend?
If not, would you like one? What do you
look for in a friend?
Any enemies? What, if so, makes them
your enemies?

LOVE: Have you ever been in Love?
Ever been out with anyone? If so, how long
was your longest relationship?
Is it important to you to have a boy/girlfriend?
What do you think makes you
Love someone?

SEX: Are you a Virgin? If not, are you
happy about it? And how old were you?
Have you Kissed anyone? Would you
describe Yourself as Heterosexual ☐,
Gay/Lesbian ☐ or Not Sure ☐.
Have you ever felt pressurised to do
something you didn't want? If so, what
happened?

YOU: If you had three wishes, what
would they be?

Are you superstitious? If so, name them.

Do you have an Idol? Who?

Do you believe in God? If so, what is your
idea of God?

♡　♡

YOU (continued)... Do you think Girls are different from boys?　If so, in what ways?

Would you describe yourself as Very Happy ☐, Happy ☐, OK ☐, Unhappy ☐ Very unhappy ☐ ?

When you have problem is there someone you can talk to?　If so, who?

If you had Loadsamoney, how would you spend it?

Do you **WORRY** a lot ☐ a little ☐ Hardly ever ☐ Not at all ☐ ?

Who do you care about most in the whole World?

Are you interested in Horoscopes?

If you could vote in the next Election, which Party would you vote for?
Why?

How would you describe your **LOOKS**?

And how would you describe your **PERSONALITY**?

Would you call yourself Black ☐ Brown ☐ Beige ☐ White ☐ or other?

LISTS: List in order of importance to you! (just use the letters!) Ⓐ Friendship Ⓑ Sex Ⓒ Sex Ⓓ Money Ⓔ Clothes Ⓕ Music Ⓖ Books Ⓗ Career Ⓘ Family Ⓙ films Ⓚ TV.

✂

♡ ♡ ♡ ♡

LIST in order of World Importance : [A] Peace
[B] The Environment [C] Starvation

And in order of National Importance : [A] Pensions
[B] Health [C] Education [D] Unemployment

AND what **WORRIES** you **MOST** ? (List letters in order).
[A] Schoolwork [B] Life at Home [C] Friendships
[D] Love [E] Sex [G] Health

**PLEASE LIST YOUR OTHER WORRIES &
COMMENTS HERE** 8 (use a separate sheet if
you want, sorry it's so cramped!)

With special Thanks to the
WANDSWORTH TEENAGE WORRIERS...

♡ cut along dotted lines and
Send to: LETTY CHUBB,   ♡
c/o CORGI, RHCB,
61-63 Uxbridge Rd
♡ LONDON W5   ♡

Thanks! Love *Letty Chubb*

Photocopy (or just cut out) this page and
send it to your MP or the PM c/o House of
Commons, LONDON S.W.1.

PETITION

WORRIERS
OF THE WORLD
UNITE!

We, the Undersigned,
ask that you immediately
consider the setting up of
a **TEENAGE THINK TANK** as outlined in

" I WAS A TEENAGE WORRIER"
(published by Corgi).

to utilize the V. Brilliant ideas
and energy of the young people
of this once great Nation.

Names	Ages	Addresses (optional)

P.T.O.

TEENAGE THINK TANK

WORRIERS
OF the WORLD
UNITE

Names	Ages	Addresses

The End
—